THE BILINGUAL BEAR

PICTURE DICTIONARY

English-Farsi Edition

نسخه انگلیسی-فارسی

Bilingual Dictionaries, Inc.

Bilingual Bear Picture Dictionary
English-Farsi Edition
1st Edition

Illustrations & Cover
Jose Quezada

Content & Design
Alex Sesma
Jose Quezada

Editor
Alex Sesma

Translation
Hessam Nejati

Publisher
Bilingual Dictionaries, Inc.

Bilingual Dictionaries, Inc.
PO Box 1154 Murrieta, CA 92564, USA
website: www.bilingualdictionaries.com email: support@bilingualdictionaries.com

ISBN13: 978-1-946986-03-0 **ISBN:** 1-946986-03-8

For information about the Bilingual Bear Picture Dictionary series and other materials visit:
website: www.BilingualBear.com

Welcome to the Bilingual Bear Picture Dictionary!

In 2015, illustrator and graphic designer Jose Quezada went to South Korea for six months to teach children English. Jose and his wife stayed in a small town called Dongtan and tutored Korean children at a private English learning school. While he probably learned less Korean than they learned English, he loved every moment of language learning with the children. As an English tutor, he was able to use his illustrations to make the children laugh and learn. The students would ask Jose to draw vocabulary on the board and in their notebooks. Jose knew he could create something special with his illustrations that would grab the children's attention in a way that was new and interesting.

We are proud to present this special picture dictionary that offers more for English language learners. Follow Benny through a bilingual story at the beginning of each chapter. Join the Bilingual Bear for activities and puzzles at the end of each chapter. We hope you and your students enjoy each and every original illustration as much as Jose loved creating them. Look out for more Bilingual Bear learning materials. This picture dictionary is just the beginning.

TABLE OF

Family 1
خانواده

Story 7
Family Members 8
Age 10
Description 11
Birthday & Wedding 21
What's Different?............. 14

Home 2
خانه

Story 15
Home & Neighbors 16
Kitchen 20
Bedroom 22
Bathroom 24
Living Room 28
Yard & Garage 30
Tools & Clean 32
Hidden Objects 34

Clothes 3
لباس ها

Story 35
Clothes 36
Shoes 37
Girls & Boys 38
Accessories 40
Style 42
Laundry 44
Benny's Maze 46

Food 4
غذا

Story 47
Food & Cook 48
Meals & Beverages 50
Breakfast & Lunch 52
Dinner 55
Dessert & Condiments ... 56
Fruits & Vegetables 58
Eat 62
Benny's Snack 64

Health 5
سلامتی

Story 65
Head..................................... 66
Body 68
Senses & Emotions 72
Sick & Hurt........................ 74
What is Different?............ 76

School 6
مدرسه

Story 77
Places & People 78
Classroom 80
Computer & Internet 82
Math & Science 84
English & Lesson 86
Supplies 88
Benny's Jet 90

CONTENTS

City 7 شهر

Story 91
Places 92
Library 94
Hospital 95
Bank 96
Public Safety 97
Auto & Traffic 98
Jobs 103
Find Benny 104

Life 8 زندگی

Story 105
Life 106
Restaurant 107
Shopping & Electronics 108
Parks 110
Sports 112
Music & Entertainment 116
Holiday 119
Hidden Objects 120

Nature 9 طبیعت

Story 121
Plants 122
Earth 124
Space & Time 126
Weather 128
Environment 131
Leaf Art 132

Animals 10 حیوانات

Story 133
Farm & Ocean 134
Forest & Jungle 136
Birds & Insects 138
Pets 140
Build Benny 142

More Words 11 کلمات بیشتر

Story 143
Numbers 144
Money 145
Time 146
Colors 147
Shapes 148

Glossary A واژه نامه

English Glossary 149

Benny's Roar

Benny is a fun bear. After school, Benny loves to play games. He loves to hug his family and laugh with his friends. Benny's mother yells, "Do your homework!" Benny roars, "Yes ROAR."

بنی خرس باحالی است. او دوست دارد که بعد از مدرسه، بازی کند. او دوست دارد که خانواده خود را بغل کند و با دوستانش بخندد. مادر بنی داد می زند: «مشق هایت را بنویس!» ، بنی داد میزند: «چشم و می غرد.

Family

Chapter 1

Benny says how he feels.

بنی درباره احساساتش حرف می زند.

His family does not understand.

خانواده اش او را درک نمی کنند.

Family

1

grandmother

2

grandfather

3

aunt

4

mother

5

father

6

uncle

7

brother

8

sister

9

cousin

1. مادربزرگ

2. پدربزرگ

3. عمه

4. مادر

5. پدر

6. دایی

7. برادر

8. خواهر

9. خاله زاده

Family

1

parents

2

children

3

husband and wife

4

son and daughter

5

niece and nephew

1. والدین
2. کودکان
3. زن و شوهر
4. پسر و دختر
5. خواهرزاده و برادرزاده

Age

1

baby

2

child

3

teenager

4

adult

5

senior

6

woman

7

girl

8

boy

9

man

1. نوزاد
2. کودک
3. نوجوان

4. بزرگسال
5. سالمند
6. زن

7. دختر
8. پسر
9. مرد

Description

1 handsome

2 pretty

3 ugly

4 thin

5 tall

6 old

7 fat

8 short

9 young

1. خوش تیپ
2. زیبا
3. زشت
4. لاغر
5. قدبلند
6. پیر
7. چاق
8. قد کوتاه
9. جوان

Birthday

1

birthday

2

cake

3

candle

4

balloon

5

gift

6

party

7

friends

8

game

9

fun

1. جشن تولد **2.** کیک **3.** شمع

4. بادکنک **5.** هدیه **6.** جشن

7. دوستان **8.** بازی **9.** سرگرمی

Wedding

1

wedding

2

bride

3

groom

4

to cry

5

to dance

6

to laugh

7

to love

8

to kiss

9

to hug

1. عروسی
2. عروس
3. داماد
4. گریه کردن
5. رقصیدن
6. خندیدن
7. عشق ورزیدن
8. بوسیدن
9. به آغوش گرفتن

What is different?

Home

Chapter 2

Benny meets new neighbors.

بنی به دیدن همسایه های جدید می رود.

They are always scared.

آنها همیشه وحشت زده اند.

Home

Home

1

house

2

apartment

3

door

4

window

5

to knock

6

doorknob

7

key

8

to ring

9

doorbell

1. منزل
2. آپارتمان
3. در
4. پنجره
5. در زدن
6. دستگیره در
7. کلید
8. زنگ زدن
9. زنگ در

Home

1

stairs

2

roof

3

chimney

4

gate

5

garage

6

fence

7

mailbox

8

mail

9

to recieve

1. پله ها
2. سقف
3. دودکش
4. دروازه
5. گاراژ
6. پرچین
7. صندوق پست
8. پست
9. دریافت کردن

Home

1

kitchen

2

bedroom

3

bathroom

4

living room

5

yard

1. آشپزخانه
2. اتاق خواب
3. حمام
4. حال پذیرایی
5. حیاط

Neighbors

1

neighbor

2

to meet

3

to invite

4

to wave

5

to play

1. همسایه
2. ملاقات کردن
3. دعوت کردن
4. دست تکان دادن
5. بازی کردن

Kitchen

1

refrigerator

2

dishwasher

3

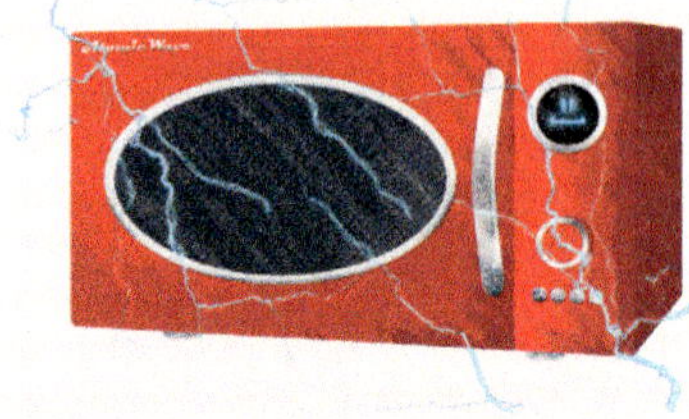

microwave

4

toaster

5

stove

6

oven

7

sink

8

counter

9

cupboard

1. یخچال
2. ماشین ظرفشویی
3. ماکروویو
4. توستر
5. فر خوراک پزی
6. اجاق
7. سینک ظرفشویی
8. میز پیشخوان
9. کابینت

Kitchen

1

plate

2

bowl

3

cup

4

knife

5

fork

6
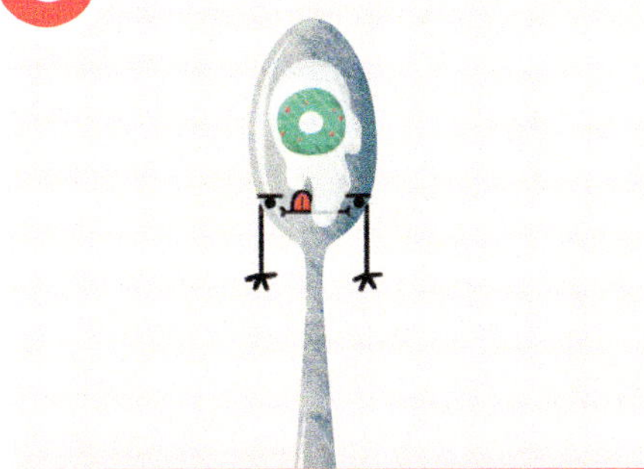
spoon

7

to prepare

8

to cook

9

to wash

1. بشقاب
2. کاسه
3. فنجان
4. چاقو
5. چنگال
6. قاشق
7. آماده کردن
8. پختن
9. شستن

Bedroom

1

bed

2

pillow

3

blanket

4

dresser

5

nightstand

6

lamp

7

closet

8

poster

9

night light

1. تخت خواب
2. بالش
3. پتو
4. میز آرایش
5. پاتختی
6. لامپ
7. کمد
8. پوستر
9. چراغ خواب

Bedroom

1

dream

2

nightmare

3

sleepy

4

awake

5

to sleep

1. رویا
2. کابوس
3. خواب آلود
4. بیدار
5. خوابیدن

Bathroom

Home

1

shower

2

bathtub

3
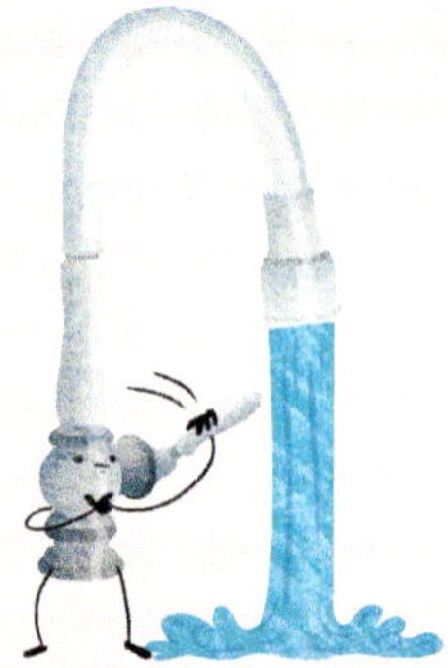

faucet

4

mirror

5

toilet

6

toilet paper

7

hamper

8

comb

9

soap

1. دوش گرفتن

2. وان حمام

3. شیر آب

4. آینه

5. توالت

6. دستمال توالت

7. زنبیل

8. شانه

9. صابون

Bathroom

1

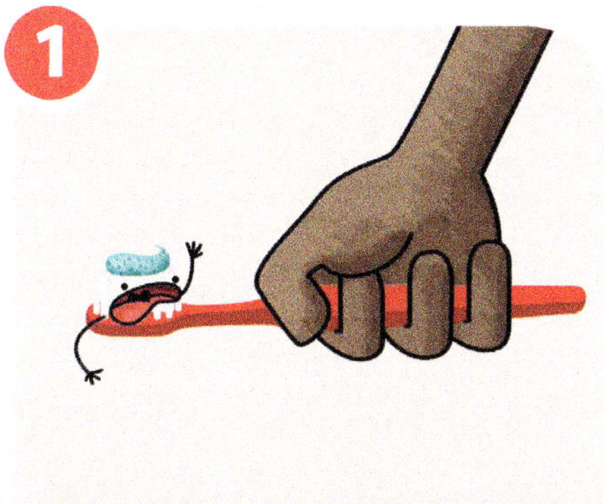

toothbrush

2

toothpaste

3

towel

4

floss

5

wet

6

dry

7

lotion

8

clean

9

dirty

1. مسواک

2. خمیردندان

3. حوله

4. نخ دندان

5. خیس

6. خشک

7. لوسیون

8. تمیز

9. کثیف

Bathroom

1

to comb

2

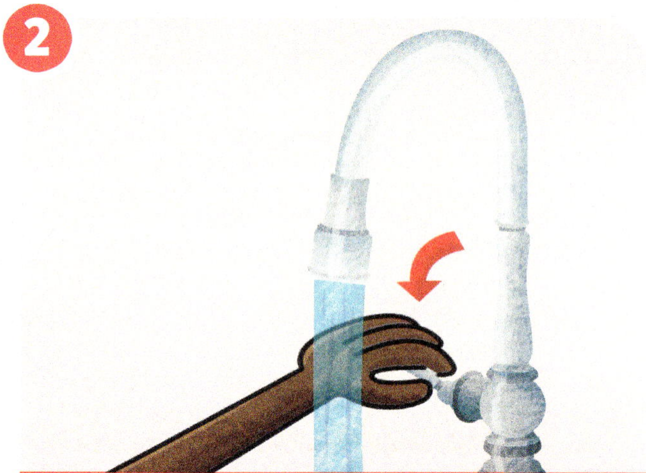

to open

3

to brush

4

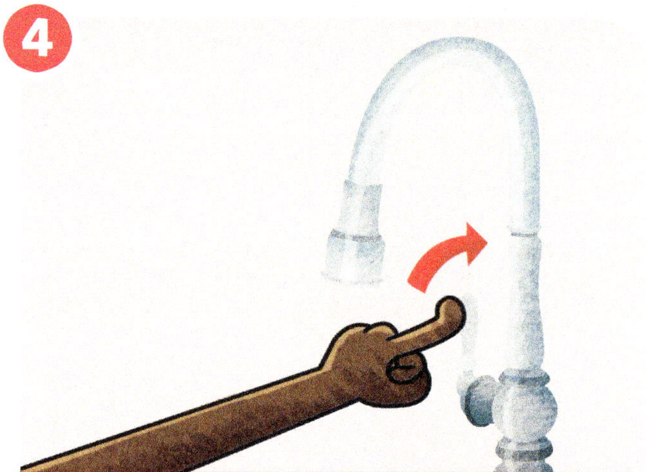

to close

5

to shower

1. شانه کردن

2. باز کردن

3. مسواک زدن

4. بستن

5. دوش گرفتن

Living Room

1

wall

2

floor

3

ceiling

4

couch

5

carpet

6

table

7

fireplace

8

painting

9

switch

1. دیوار
2. کف زمین
3. سقف
4. مبل راحتی
5. فرش
6. میز
7. شومینه
8. تابلو نقاشی
9. کلید برق

Living Room

1

television

2

DVD player

3

radio

4

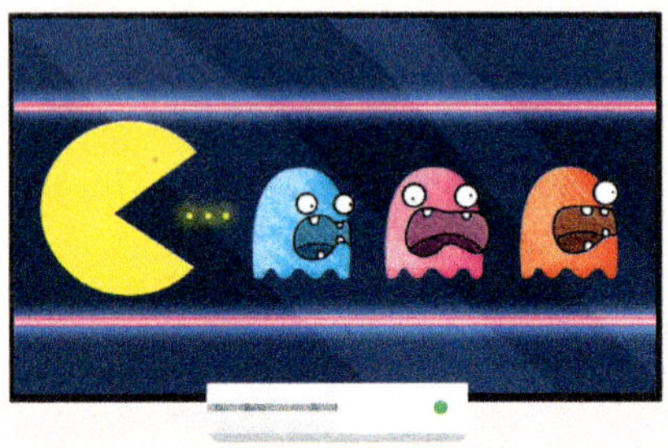

video game

5

controller

6

toy

7

board game

8

off

9

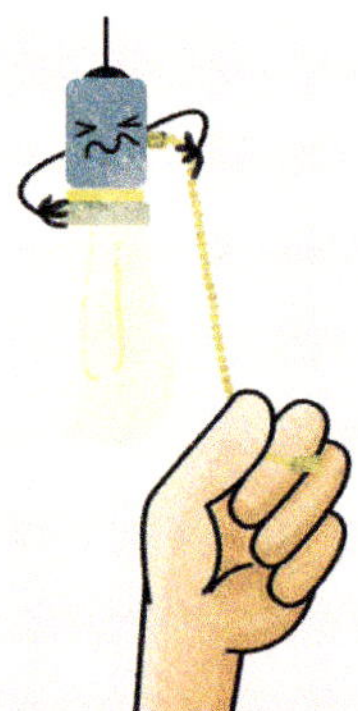

on

1. تلویزیون
2. دستگاه دی وی دی
3. رادیو
4. بازی ویدیویی
5. کنترل از راه دور
6. اسباب بازی
7. صفحه بازی
8. خاموش
9. روشن

Living Room

1

together

2

to cheer

3

alone

4

to watch

5

comfortable

1. با هم دیگر
2. خوشحالی کردن
3. تنها
4. تماشا کردن
5. راحت

Home

Yard

1

lawn

2

garden

3

barbecue

4

lawn mower

5

trash can

6
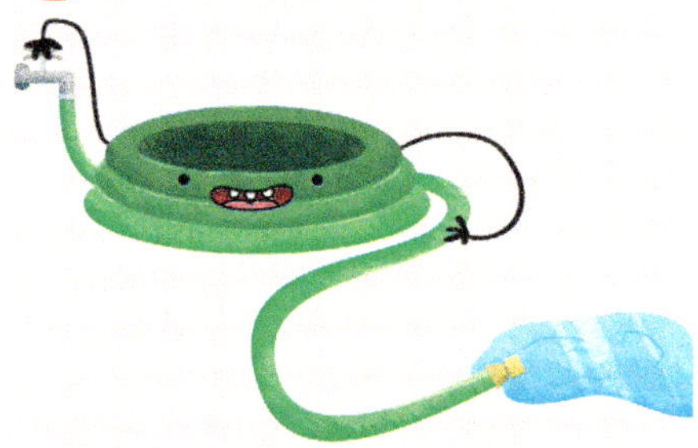
hose

7

dog house

8

tree house

9
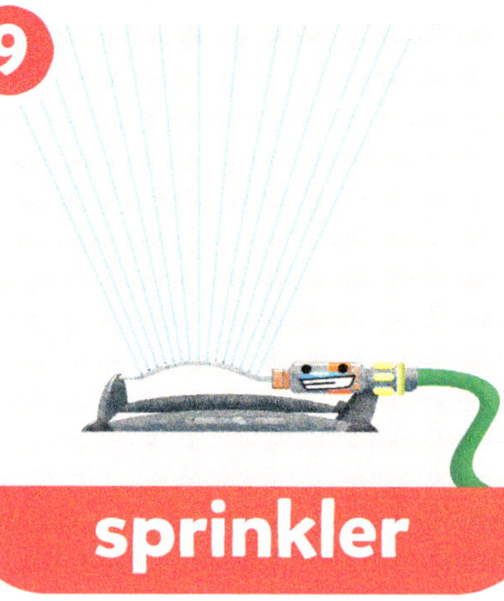
sprinkler

1. چمن
2. باغچه
3. باربیکیو
4. ماشین چمن زنی
5. سطل زباله
6. شلنگ
7. لانه سگ
8. خانه درختی
9. آب پاش

Garage

1

paint

2

ladder

3

cooler

4

fan

5

recycle bin

6

bag

7

to carry

8

box

9

to fall

1. نقاشی
2. نردبان
3. کولر
4. پنکه
5. سطل آشغال
6. کیسه
7. حمل کردن
8. جعبه
9. افتادن

Tools

1

hammer

2

nail

3

screwdriver

4

power drill

5

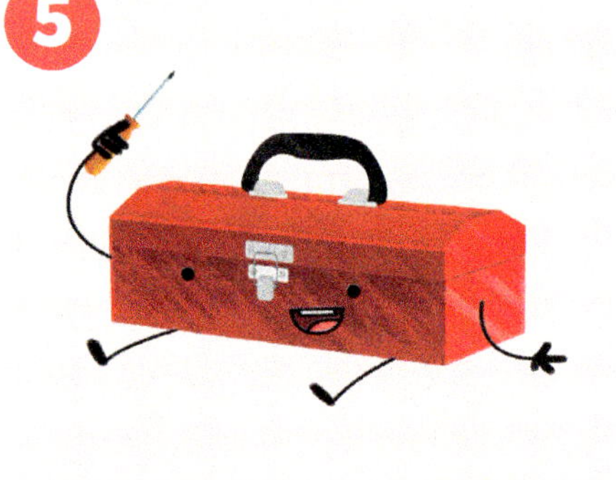

toolbox

6

wrench

7

to break

8

tape

9

to fix

1. چکش

2. میخ

3. پیچ گوشتی

4. دریل قدرتی

5. جعبه ابزار

6. آچار فرانسه

7. شکستن

8. نوارچسب

9. تعمیر کردن

Clean

1

broom

2

dustpan

3

mop

4

sponge

5

vaccum

6

bucket

7

to sweep

8

to scrub

9

to empty

1. جارو

2. خاک انداز

3. گردگیری

4. اسفنج

5. جارو برقی

6. سطل

7. جارو کردن

8. سابیدن

9. خالی کردن

Find the Object

Home

Benny needs new shoes for school.

بنی به کفش های جدید برای مدرسه نیاز دارد.

Heels are not his style.

کفش های پاشنه بلند سبک او نیستند.

Clothes

Clothes

1

shirt

2

pants

3

shorts

4

underwear

5

sock

6

shoes

7

sweater

8

jacket

9

hat

1. پیراهن
2. شلوار
3. شورت
4. لباس زیر
5. جوراب
6. کفش
7. پلیور
8. ژاکت
9. کلاه

Shoes

1

sandals

2

boots

3

sneakers

4

heel

5

sole

6
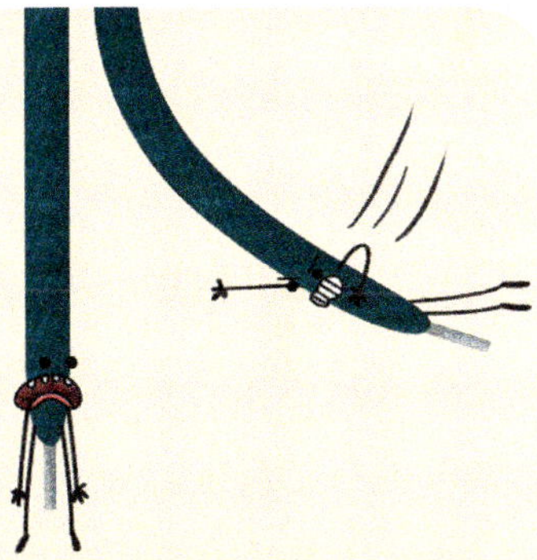
shoelaces

7

to tie

8

to put on

9

to take off

1. صندل
2. چکمه
3. کتانی
4. پاشنه بلند
5. پاشنه تخت
6. بند کفش
7. گره زدن
8. پوشیدن
9. بیرون آوردن

Girls

1

dress

2

skirt

3

bikini

4

make-up

5

purse

1. پیراهن
2. دامن
3. مایو دو تکه
4. آرایش کردن
5. کیف پول

Boys

1

jeans

2

t-shirt

3

baseball cap

4

swimming trunks

5

wallet

1. شلوار جین

2. تی شرت

3. کلاه بیسبال

4. مایوی مردانه

5. کیف پول

Accessories

1

belt

2

scarf

3

watch

4

zipper

5

button

6
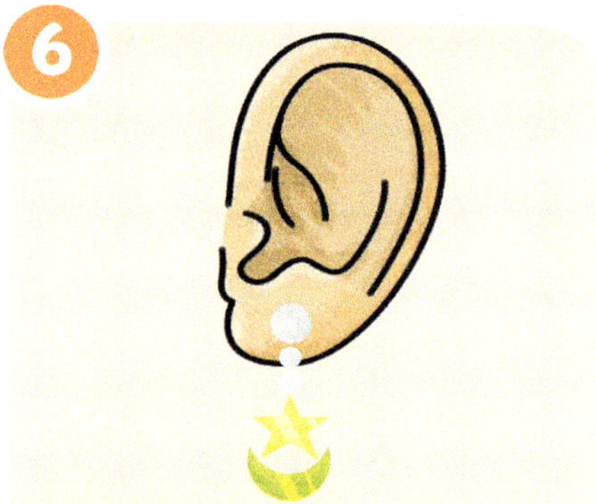
earring

7

ring

8

necklace

9

bracelet

1. کمربند	2. شال	3. ساعت
4. زیپ	5. دکمه	6. گوشواره
7. انگشتر	8. گردنبند	9. دستبند

Accessories

1

uniform

2
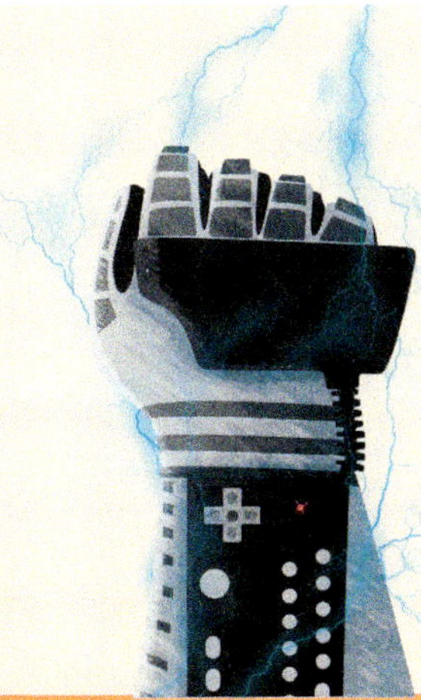
glove

3

cowboy hat

4

costume

5

pajamas

1. لباس فرم
2. دستکش
3. کلاه کابوی
4. لباس مراسم
5. پیژامه

Style

1

solid

2

striped

3

polka dot

4

small

5

medium

6

torn

7

large

8

extra large

9

stained

1. ساده
2. راه راه
3. نقطه نقطه
4. کوچک
5. متوسط
6. پاره
7. بزرگ
8. بسیار بزرگ
9. رنگی رنگی

Style

1

new

2

used

3

tight

4

loose

1. جدید
2. دست دوم
3. تنگ
4. گشاد
5. سبک

5

style

Laundry

1

dryer

2

washer

3

detergent

4

basket

5

laundry

6

hanger

7

iron

8

to iron

9

wrinkled

1. ماشین خشک کن
2. ماشین لباسشویی
3. مایع لباسشویی
4. سبد
5. لباس
6. جا رختی
7. اتو
8. اتو کردن
9. چروک شده

Laundry

1

to try

2

to wear

3

to fold

4

to put

1. امتحان کردن

2. پوشیدن

3. تا کردن

4. گذاشتن

5. آویزان کردن

5

to hang

Benny's Maze

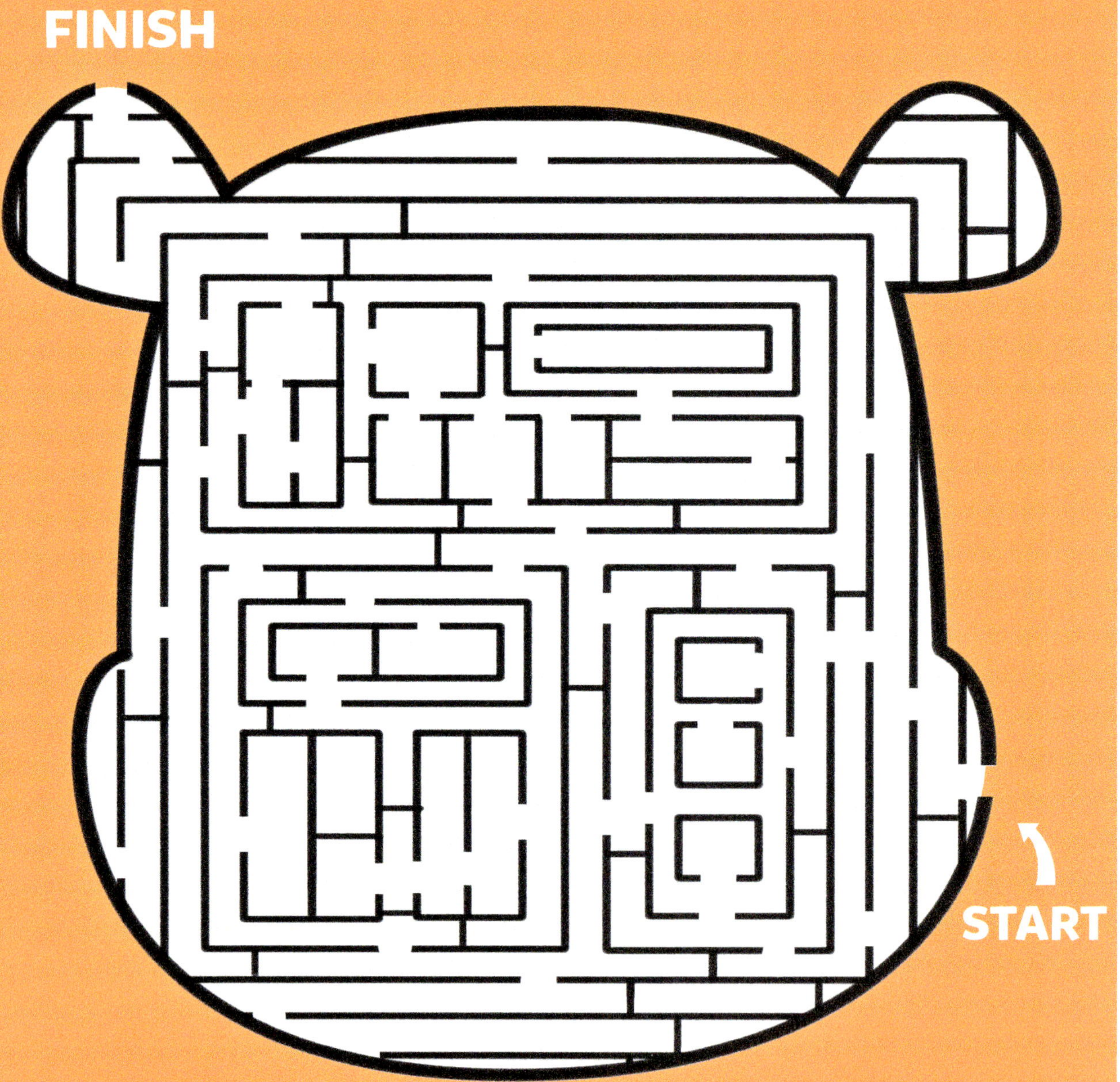

Food

Chapter 4

Benny orders pizza for lunch.

بنی برای ناهار پیتزا سفارش می دهد.

He only eats pancakes for breakfast.

او صبحانه فقط پنکیک می خورد.

Food

1

fruit

2

vegetable

3

meat

4

bread

5

condiments

1. میوه

2. سبزیجات

3. گوشت

4. نان

5. چاشنی

Cook

1

pan

2

pot

3

to grill

4

to peel

5

to stir

6

to boil

7

to fry

8

to bake

9

to blend

1. تابه
2. دیگ
3. بریان کردن
4. پوست کردن
5. هم زدن
6. جوشاندن
7. سرخ کردن
8. پختن
9. مخلوط کردن

Food

Meals

Food

1

breakfast

2

lunch

3

dinner

4

beverage

5

dessert

1. صبحانه

2. ناهار

3. شام

4. نوشیدنی

5. دسر

Beverages

1

juice

2

milk

3

thirsty

4

soda

5

lemonade

6

water

7

coffee

8

tea

9

ice

1. آبمیوه
2. شیر
3. تشنه
4. نوشابه
5. لیموناد
6. آب
7. قهوه
8. چای
9. یخ

Breakfast

Food

1

egg

2

bacon

3

sausage

4

butter

5

pancakes

6
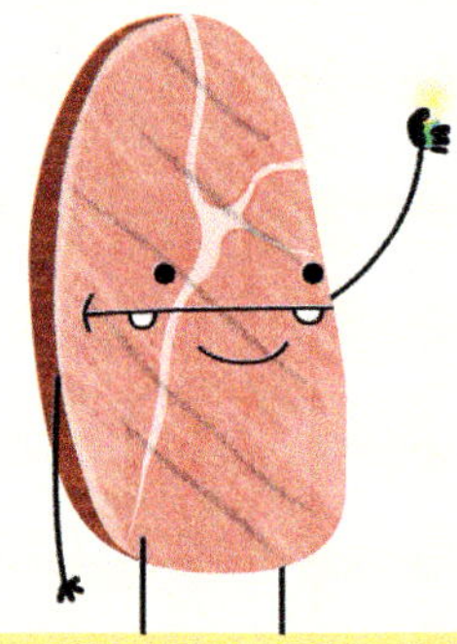
ham

7

oatmeal

8

cereal

9

toast

1. تخم مرغ
2. بیکن
3. سوسیس
4. کره
5. پنکیک
6. ژامبون گوشت
7. بلغور جو
8. غلات صبحانه
9. نان تست

Lunch

1

fries

2

hamburger

3

hotdog

4

chicken nugget

5

pizza

6

corndog

7

sandwich

8

burrito

9

fish sticks

1. سیب زمینی سرخ کرده
2. همبرگر
3. هات داگ
4. ناگت مرغ
5. پیتزا
6. هات داگ ذرت
7. ساندویچ
8. بوریتو
9. ناگت ماهی

Lunch

Food

1

lunch box

2

cheese

3

4

peanut butter

jelly

5

snacks

1. ظرف غذا

2. پنیر

3. کره بادام زمینی

4. ژله

5. اسنک

Dinner

1

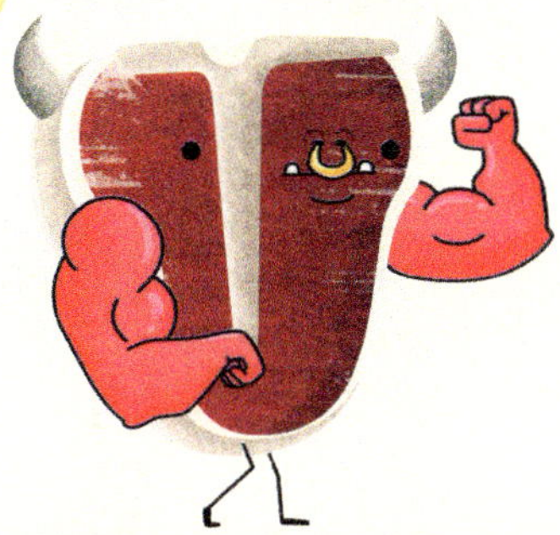

steak

2

chicken

3

sushi

4

soup

5

spaghetti

6

salad

7

beans

8

rice

9

tortilla

1. استیک
2. مرغ
3. سوشی
4. سوپ
5. اسپاگتی
6. سالاد
7. لوبیا
8. برنج
9. تورتیلا

Dessert

1

junk food

2

chips

3

cookie

4

donut

5

pie

6

cupcake

7

frosting

8

ice cream

9

chocolate

1. هله هوله
2. چیپس
3. بیسکوئیت
4. دونات
5. کلوچه
6. کیک فنجانی
7. کیک خامه ای
8. بستنی
9. شکلات

Condiments

1

ketchup

2

barbeque sauce

3

salad dressing

4

mustard

5

mayonnaise

6

salt

7

to dip

8

to pour

9

to sprinkle

1. سس کچاپ
2. سس باربیکیو
3. سس سالاد
4. خردل
5. مایونز
6. نمک
7. فرو بردن
8. ریختن
9. پاشیدن

Fruit

Food

1

apple

2

banana

3

grapes

4

pineapple

5

strawberry

6

watermelon

7

pumpkin

8

avocado

9

blueberry

1. سیب
2. موز
3. انگور
4. آناناس
5. توت فرنگی
6. هندوانه
7. کدو تنبل
8. آواکادو
9. بلوبری

Fruit

1
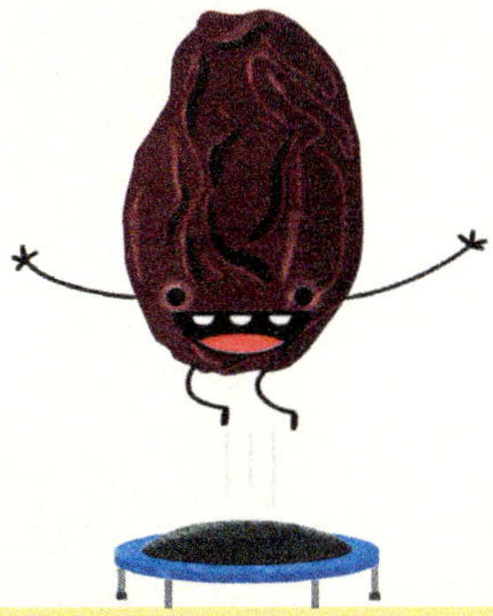
raisin

2

orange

3

mango

4

coconut

5

lemon

6

lime

7

sliced

8

juicy

9

cherry

1. کشمش
2. پرتقال
3. انبه
4. نارگیل
5. لیمو
6. لیمو ترش
7. قاچ شده
8. آبدار
9. گیلاس

Vegetables

Food

1
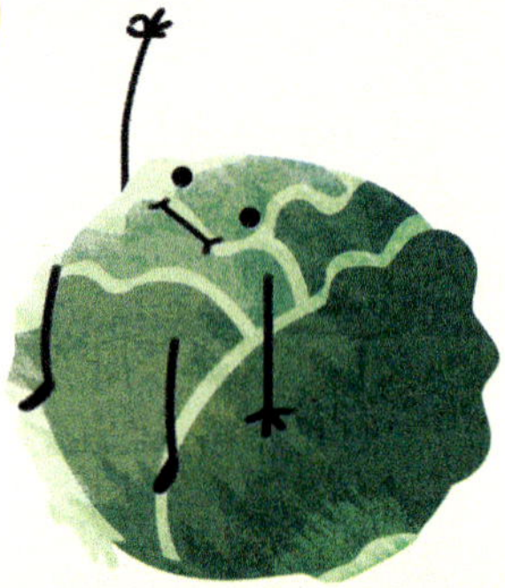
lettuce

2

celery

3

carrot

4

tomato

5

onion

6

cucumber

7

mushroom

8

broccoli

9

pickle

1. کاهو
2. کرفس
3. هویج
4. گوجه فرنگی
5. پیاز
6. خیار
7. قارچ
8. بروکلی
9. خیارشور

Vegetables

Food

1

processed

2

organic

3

rotten

4

ripe

5

fresh

1. فرآوری شده
2. ارگانیک
3. فاسد
4. رسیده
5. تازه

Eat

Food

1

to eat

2

to chew

3

to drink

4

to lick

5

to burp

1. خوردن

2. جویدن

3. نوشیدن

4. لیس زدن

5. آروغ زدن

Eat

1

spicy

2

hungry

3

sweet

4

delicious

5

full

1. گرسنه
2. گشنه
3. شیرین
4. خوشمزه
5. سیر

Benny's Snack

What you'll need!

- Bread
- Peanut Butter
- Sliced Cheese
- Organic Strawberries

1. Wash the strawberries and slice the tops off.
2. Put peanut butter and cheese on the bread. Toast the bread.
3. Put sliced strawberries on the bread and enjoy.

Fun Fact: Benny eats three full meals a day. He eats lots of meat, vegetables and drinks a lot of water!

Health

Chapter 5

Benny goes to the doctor when he is sick.

بنی هر وقت مریض می شود به پزشک مراجعه می کند.

He only has a stomachache.

او فقط دل درد دارد.

Head

1

head

2

hair

3

face

4

eye

5

eyebrow

6
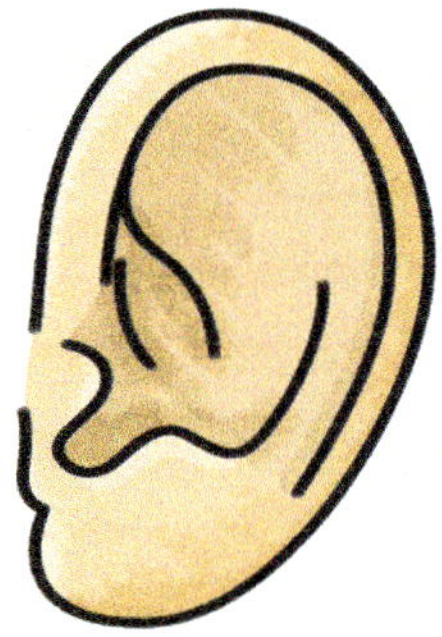
ear

7
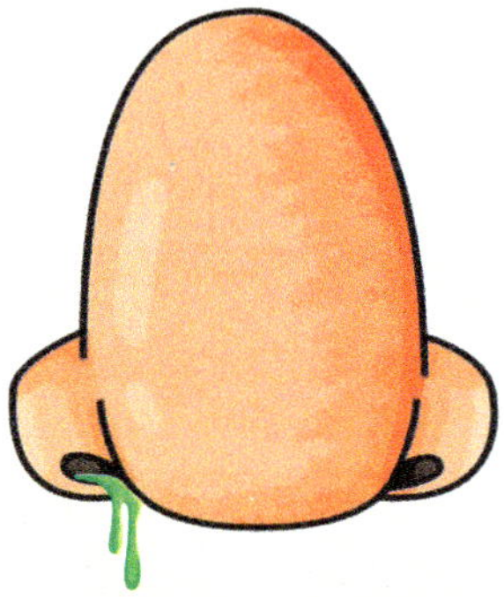
nose

8

forehead

9

cheek

Health

1. سر
2. مو
3. صورت
4. چشم
5. ابرو
6. گوش
7. بینی
8. پیشانی
9. لپ

Head

1

mouth

2

teeth

3
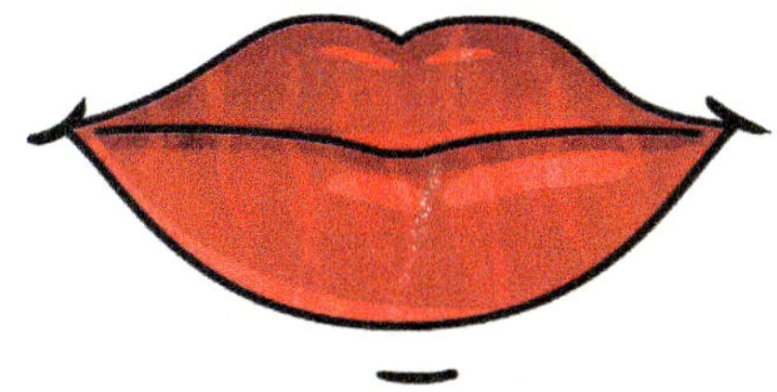
lips

4
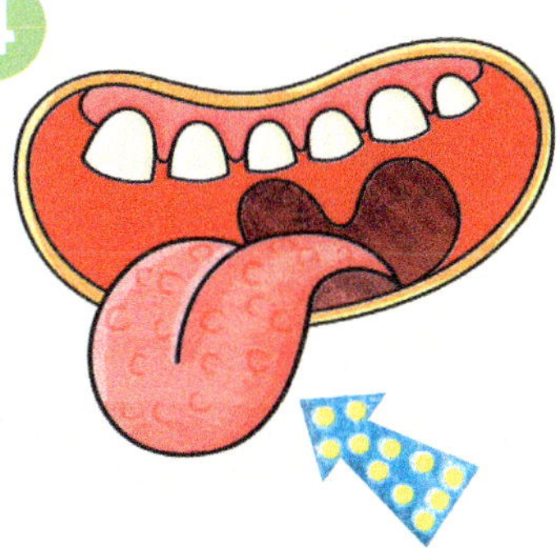
tongue

5

chin

6

neck

7
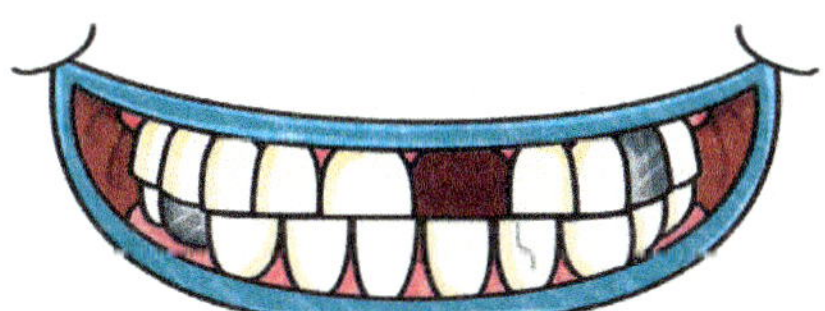
to smile

8
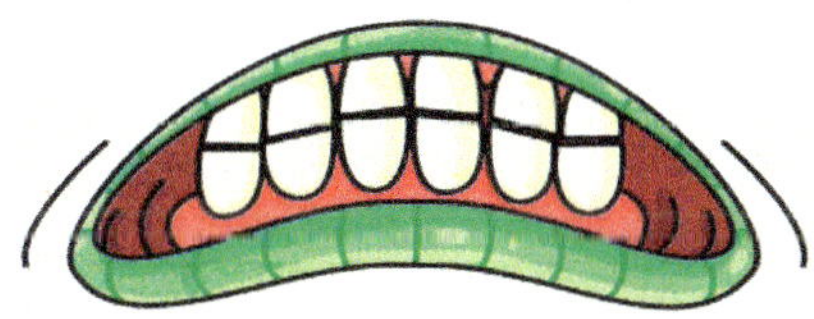
to bite

9

to wink

1. دهان
2. دندان
3. لب
4. زبان
5. چانه
6. گردن
7. لبخند زدن
8. گاز گرفتن
9. چشمک زدن

Body

1
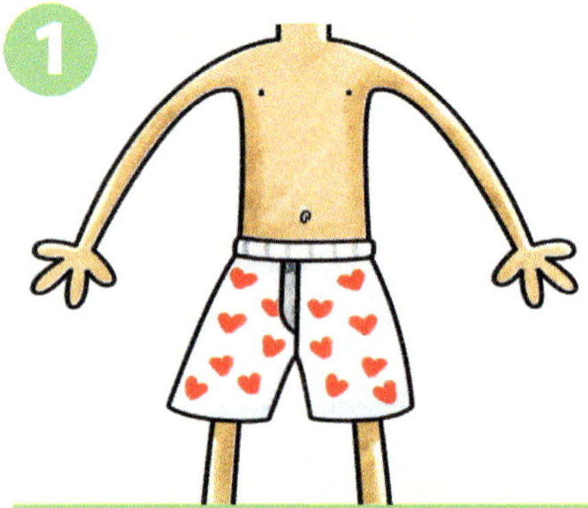

body

2

shoulder

3
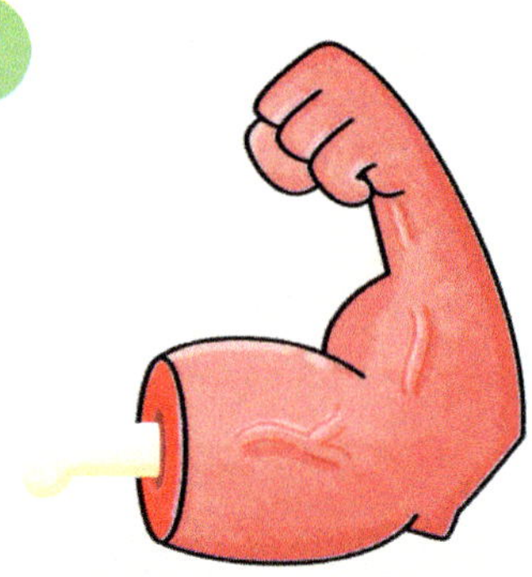

arm

4
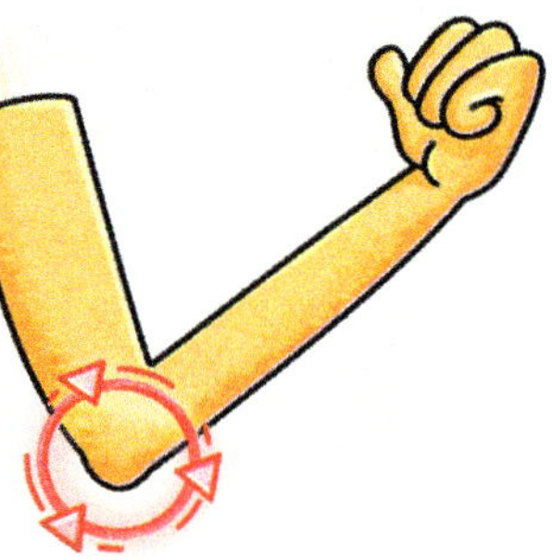

elbow

5

wrist

6
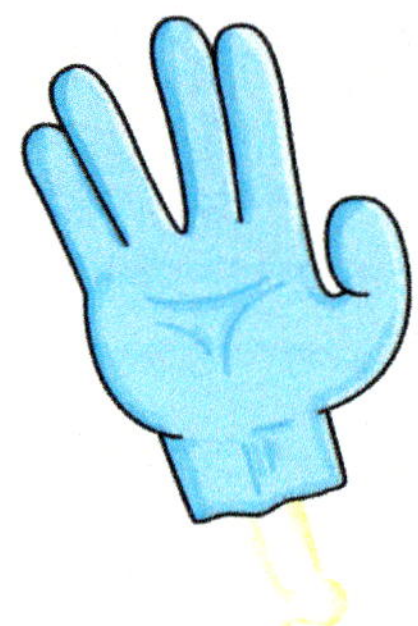

hand

7

finger

8

thumb

9

nail

1. بدن
2. شانه
3. بازو
4. آرنج
5. مچ دست
6. دست
7. انگشت
8. انگشت شست
9. ناخن

Body

1
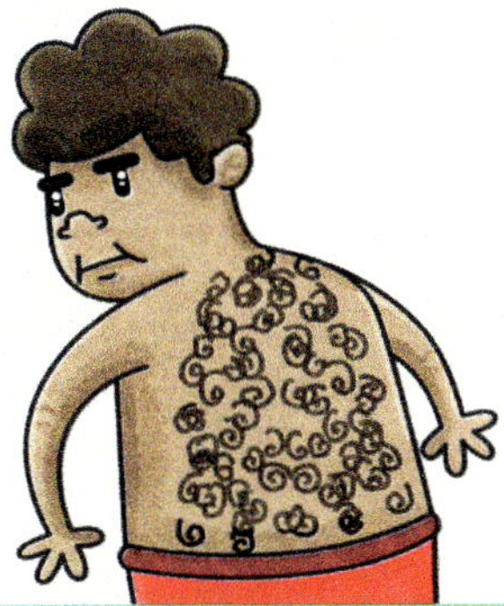
back

2

chest

3

hips

4
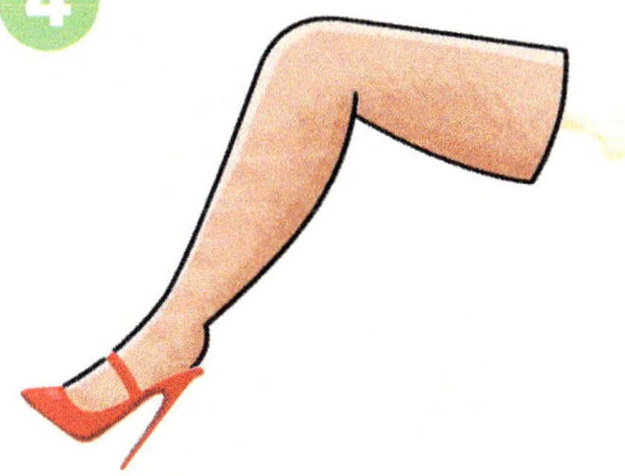
leg

5

knee

6
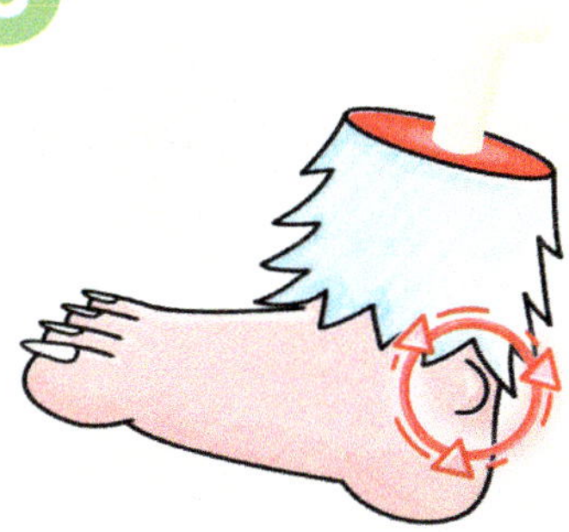
ankle

7
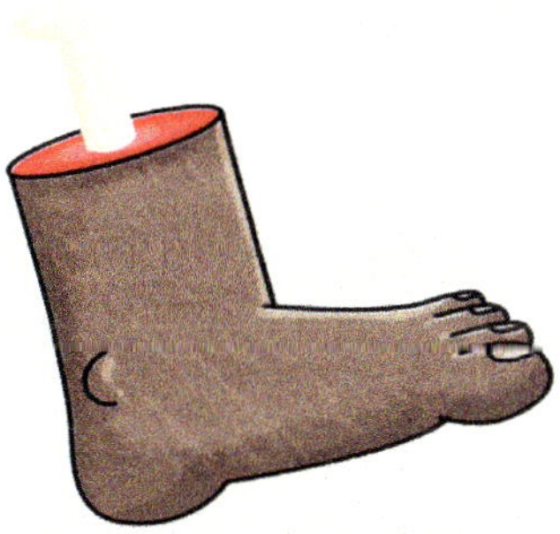
foot

8
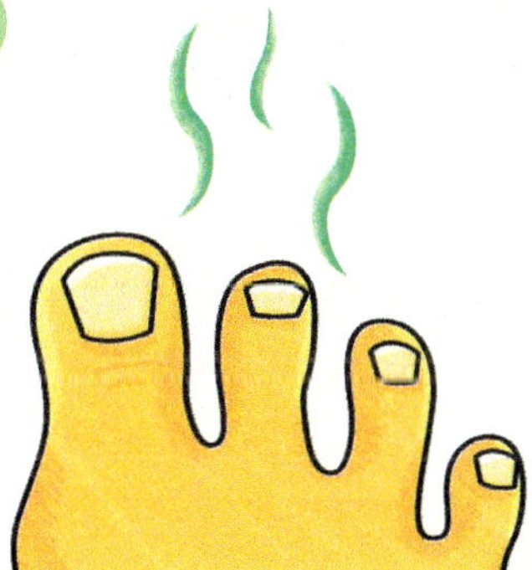
toe

9

healthy

Health

1. پشت
2. سینه
3. باسن
4. پا
5. زانو
6. مچ پا
7. پا
8. انگشت پا
9. سالم

Body

Health

1

brain

2

to think

3
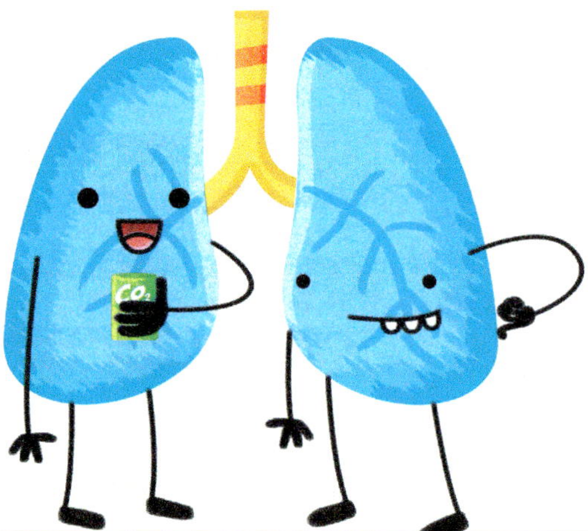

lungs

4

to breathe

5

stomach

1. مغز
2. فکر کردن
3. شش ها
4. نفس کشیدن
5. معده

Body

1

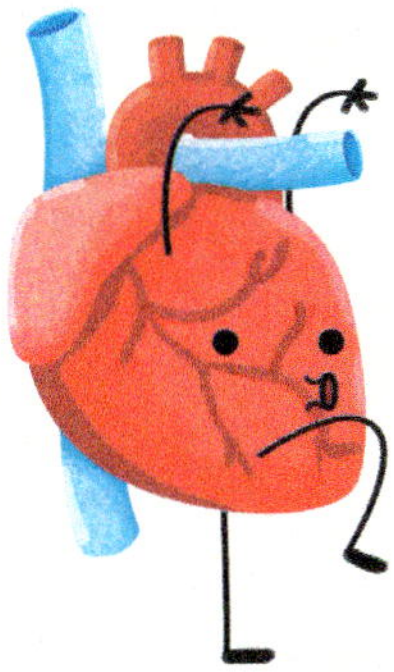

heart

2

blood

3

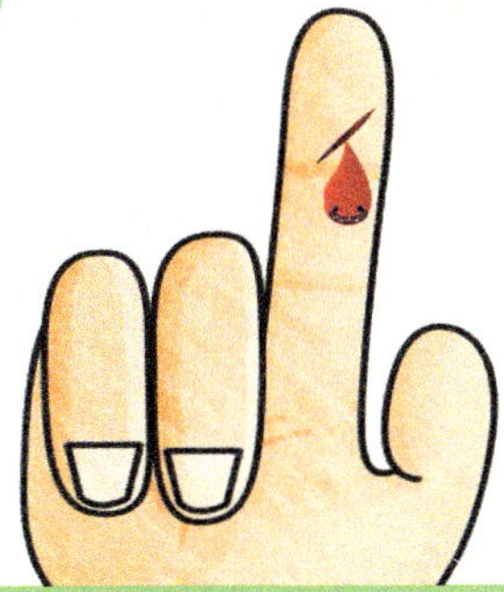

to bleed

4

muscle

5

strong

6

weak

7

bone

8

skull

9

skeleton

Health

1. قلب
2. خون
3. خونریزی کردن
4. ماهیچه
5. قوی
6. ضعیف
7. استخوان
8. جمجمه
9. اسکلت

Senses

1

to see

2

to hear

3

to taste

4

to smell

5

to touch

1. دیدن
2. شنیدن
3. چشیدن
4. بوییدن
5. لمس کردن

Emotions

1

happy

2

sad

3

scared

4

angry

5

surprised

6

excited

7

embarrassed

8

proud

9

shy

Health

1. خوشحال
2. ناراحت
3. ترسیده
4. عصبانی
5. متعجب
6. هیجان زده
7. خجالت زده
8. مغرور
9. خجالتی

Sick

1

cold

2

fever

3

flu

4

to cough

5

to sneeze

6

headache

7

allergy

8

to vomit

9

stomach ache

Health

1. سرما خوردگی
2. تب
3. آنفولانزا
4. سرفه کردن
5. عطسه کردن
6. سردرد
7. حساسیت
8. استفراغ کردن
9. دل درد

Hurt

1 **cut**

2 **bruise**

3 **burn**

4 **rash**

5 **pain**

6 **bloody** *(nose)*

7 **sprained** *(ankle)*

8 **swollen** *(finger)*

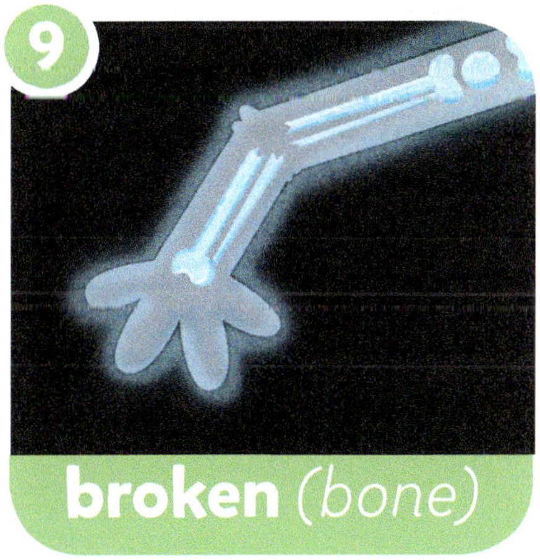

9 **broken** *(bone)*

1. بریدگی
2. کبودی
3. سوختگی
4. خارش
5. درد
6. خونین
7. رگ به رگ
8. متورم
9. شکسته

What's Different?

Benny answers the question.

بنی پاسخ سوال را می دهد.

He does not pass the test.

او امتحان را قبول نمی شود.

Places

1

office

2

classroom

3

cafeteria

4

field

5

auditorium

6

gymnasium

7

playground

8

fountain

9

locker

1. دفتر کار
2. کلاس
3. کافه تریا
4. مزرعه
5. تالار کنفرانس
6. ورزشگاه
7. زمین بازی
8. آب نما
9. قفسه قفل دار

People

1

principal

2

teacher

3

student

4

janitor

5

nurse

6

classmate

7

guard

8

to respect

9

to listen

1. مدیر مدرسه
2. معلم
3. دانش آموز
4. سرایدار
5. پرستار
6. همکلاسی
7. نگهبان
8. احترام گذاشتن
9. گوش کردن

Classroom

School

1

whiteboard

2

marker

3

desk

4

projector

5

screen

6

flag

7

clock

8

quiet

9

loud

1. تخته وایت برد
2. ماژیک
3. نیمکت
4. دستگاه پروژکتور
5. صفحه نمایش
6. پرچم
7. ساعت
8. سکوت
9. شلوغ

Classroom

1

to teach

2

bus

3

elementary

4

middle school

5

high school

6

college

7

to study

8

to learn

9

to graduate

1. درس دادن
2. اتوبوس
3. ابتدایی
4. مدرسه راهنمایی
5. دبیرستان
6. کالج
7. درس خواندن
8. یاد گرفتن
9. فارغ التحصیل شدن

Computer

School

1 computer

2 laptop

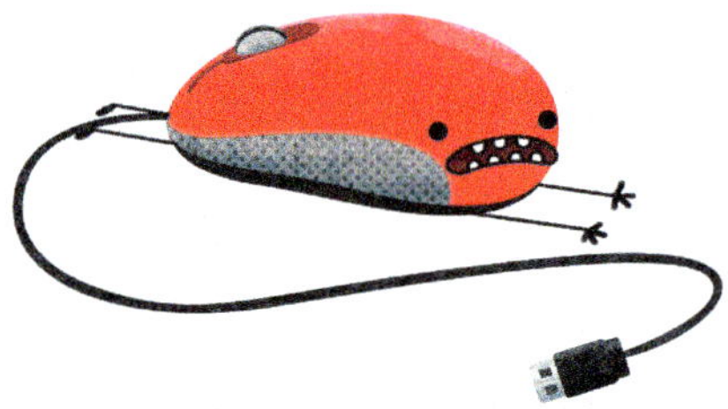

3 mouse

4 monitor

5 keyboard

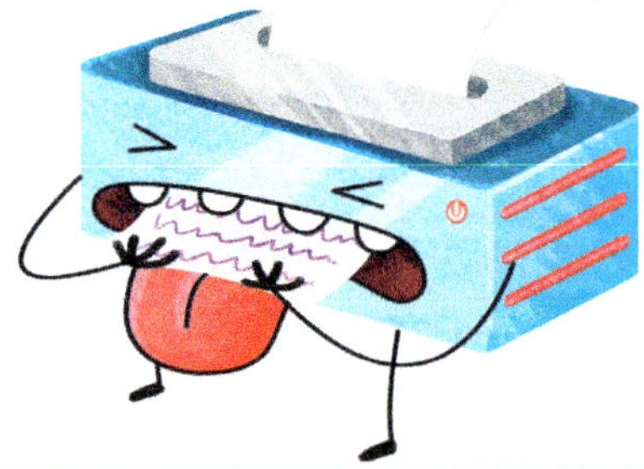

6 printer

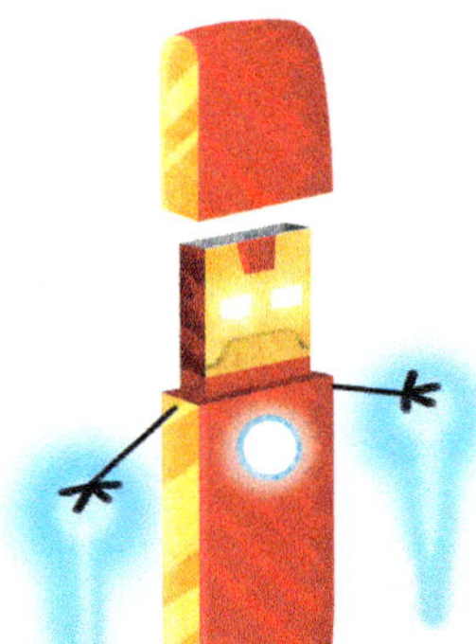

7 flash drive

8 usb port

9 speaker

1. رایانه
2. لپ تاپ
3. ماوس
4. مانیتور
5. کیبورد
6. پرینتر
7. فلش درایو
8. پورت USB
9. بلندگو

Internet

1 internet

2 browser

3 website

4 username

5 password

6 link

7 to login

8 email

9 to search

1. اینترنت
2. صفحه مرورگر
3. وبسایت
4. نام کاربری
5. رمز عبور
6. لینک
7. وارد شدن
8. ایمیل
9. جستجو کردن

Math

1

math

2

to add

3

to subtract

4

calculator

5

to multiply

6

to divide

7

graph

8

odd

9

even

1. ریاضی
2. جمع کردن
3. تفریق کردن
4. ماشین حساب
5. ضرب کردن
6. تقسیم کردن
7. گراف
8. عدد فرد
9. عدد زوج

Science

1

science

2

experiment

3

scientist

4

data

5

atom

6
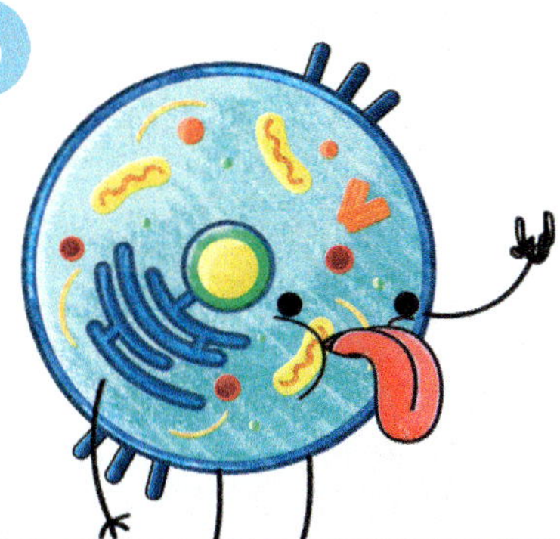
cell

7

to observe

8

electricity

9

energy

1. علم
2. تجربه
3. دانشمند
4. داده
5. اتم
6. سلول
7. مشاهده کردن
8. الکتریسیته
9. انرژی

English

1

language

2

alphabet

3

question

4

letter

5

word

6

sentence

7

to write

8

to type

9

to read

1. زبان
2. حروف الفبا
3. سوال

4. حرف
5. کلمه
6. جمله

7. نوشتن
8. تایپ کردن
9. خواندن

Lesson

1

lesson

2

homework

3

test

4

report

5

textbook

6

easy

7

to turn-in

8

to forget

9

difficult

1. درس
2. مشق
3. امتحان
4. گزارش
5. کتاب درسی
6. آسان
7. ارائه دادن
8. فراموش کردن
9. سخت

Supplies

School

1

pencil

2

pen

3

crayon

4

backpack

5

paper

6

eraser

7

scissors

8

glue

9

ruler

1. مداد
2. خودکار
3. مدادشمعی
4. کوله پشتی
5. کاغذ
6. پاک کن
7. قیچی
8. چسب مایع
9. خط کش

Supplies

1

to color

2

to glue

3

to erase

4

to cut

5

to measure

1. رنگ کردن

2. چسب زدن

3. پاک کردن

4. بریدن

5. اندازه گرفتن

Benny's Jet

Download Benny's Jet:
www.bilingualbear.com

1. Fold corners 1 and 2 along the vertical line.

2. Fold corner 3 down so you can see Benny.

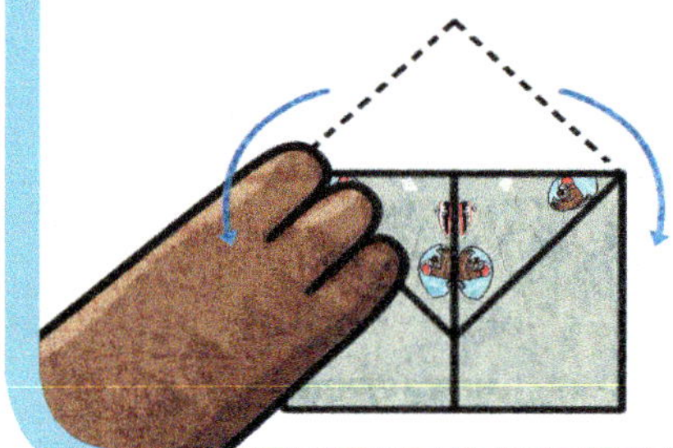

3. Fold corners 4 and 5 to match Benny's face.

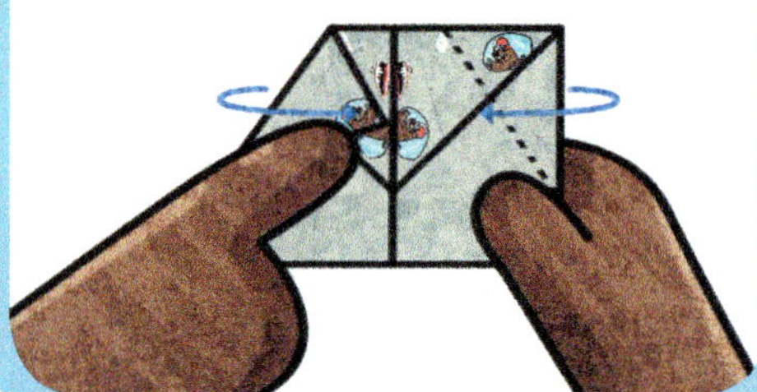

4. Fold triangle 6 up on top of corners 4 and 5.

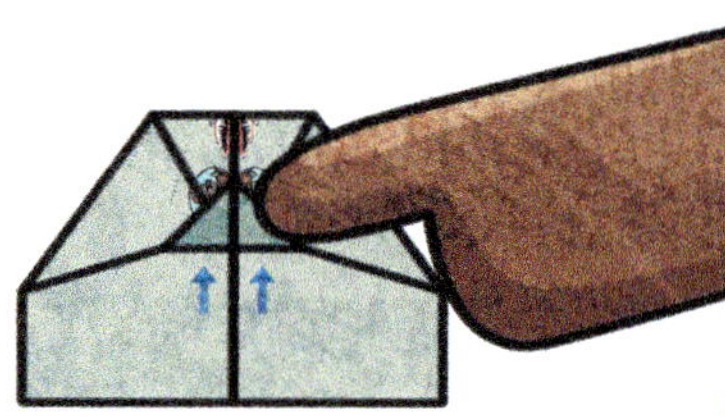

5. Flip the paper over and fold the jet in half.

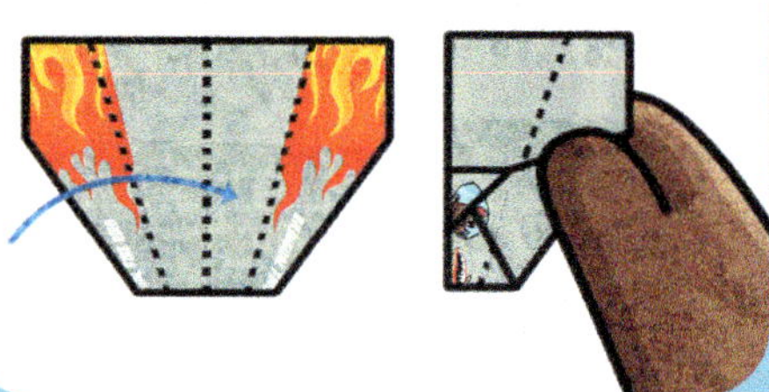

6. Fold wings 7 and 8 down along the dotted line.

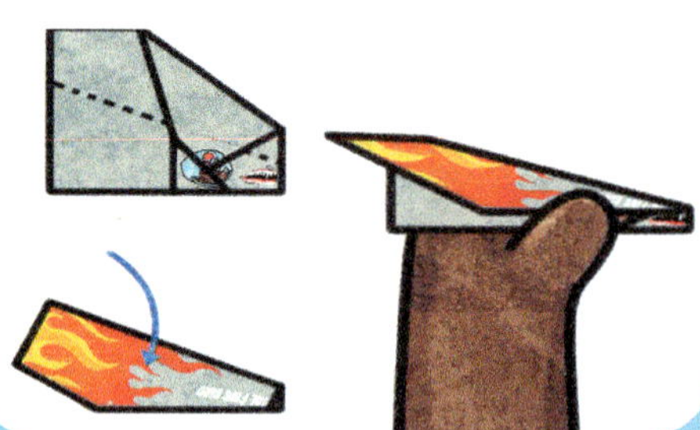

City

Chapter 7

Benny looks for the arcade.

بنی دنبال یک آرکید می گردد.

This game is no fun.

بازی اصلا سرگرم کننده نیست.

Places

1

city

2

church

3

post office

4

police station

5

fire station

6
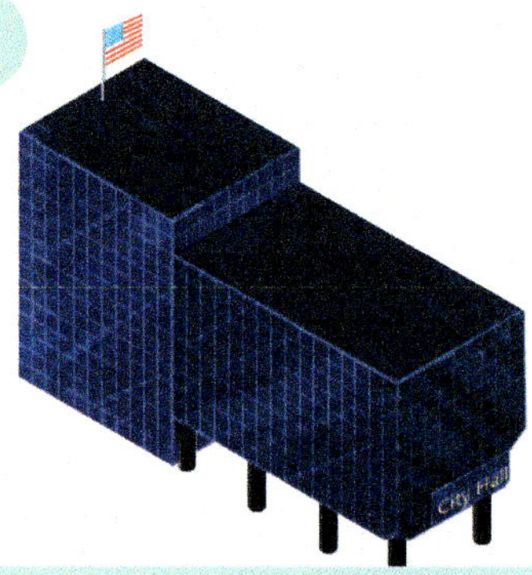

city hall

7
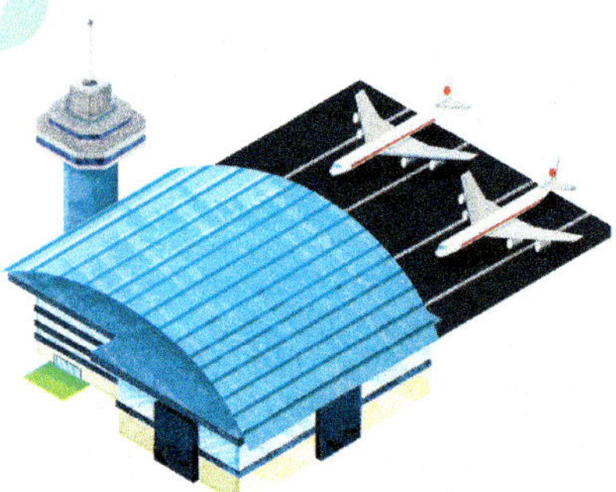
airport

8
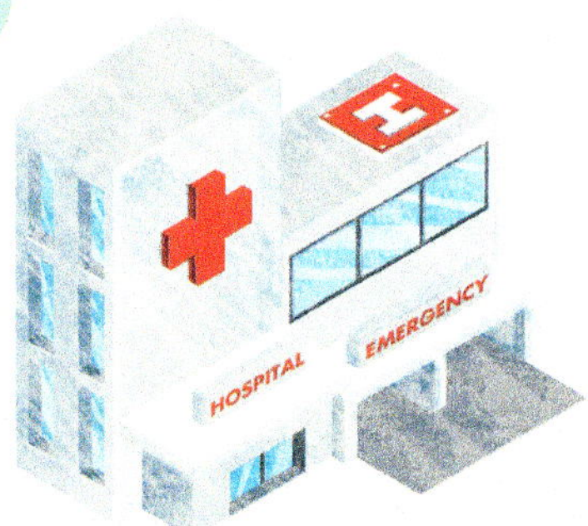

hospital

9

library

1. شهر
2. کلیسا
3. اداره پست
4. اداره پلیس
5. ایستگاه آتش نشانی
6. تالار شهر
7. فرودگاه
8. بیمارستان
9. کتابخانه

Places

1

gas station

2

parking lot

3

bus stop

4

auto shop

5

court house

6

bank

7

bridge

8

museum

9

tunnel

City

1. پمپ بنزین
2. پارکینگ
3. ایستگاه اتوبوس
4. گالری فروش خودرو
5. دادگاه
6. بانک
7. پل
8. موزه
9. تونل

Library

1

librarian

2

library card

3

book

4

author

5

title

6

magazine

7

to check out

8

to return

9

newspaper

1. کتابدار
2. کارت عضویت کتابخانه
3. کتاب
4. نویسنده
5. موضوع
6. مجله
7. به امانت گرفتن
8. بازگرداندن
9. روزنامه

Hospital

1

doctor

2

patient

3

dentist

4

medicine

5

crutch

6

x-ray

7
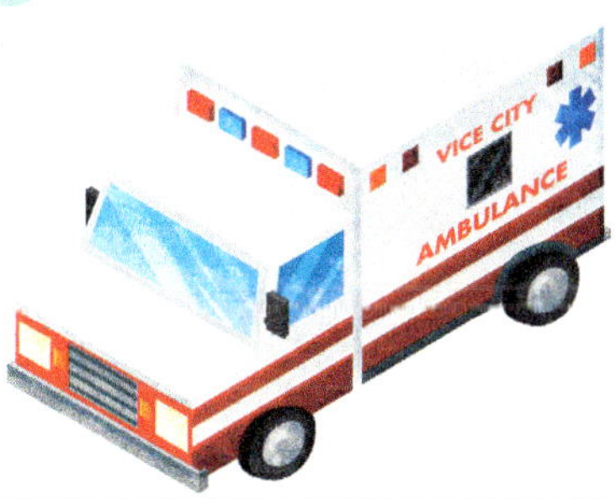

ambulance

8

emergency

9
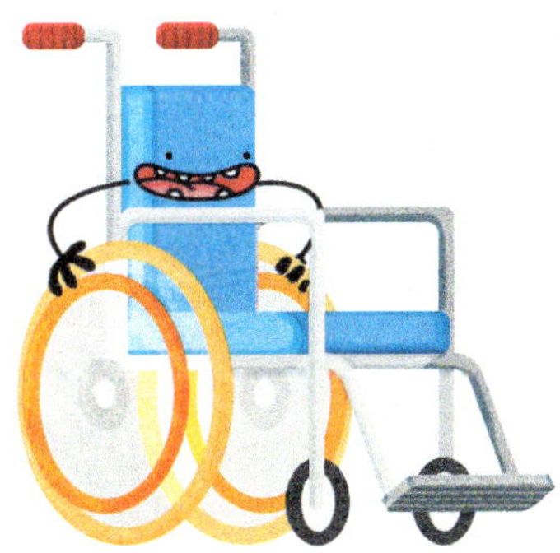
wheelchair

1. پزشک
2. بیمار
3. دندان پزشک
4. دارو
5. عصای زیر بغل
6. اشعه ایکس
7. آمبولانس
8. اورژانس
9. صندلی چرخدار

Bank

1

teller

2

money

3

dollar

4

check

5

debit card

6

pin number

7
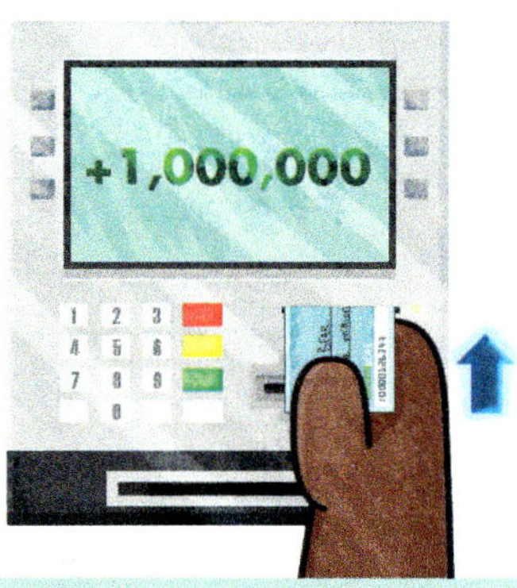

to deposit

8

to withdraw

9

to save

1. کارمند بانک
2. پول
3. دلار
4. چک
5. کارت بانکی
6. رمز پین
7. سپرده گذاری کردن
8. برداشت کردن
9. پس انداز کردن

City

Public Safety

1

police car

2

crime

3

police officer

4

fire truck

5

fire

6

fire fighter

7

tank

8

freedom

9

soldier

1. ماشین پلیس
2. جرم
3. افسر پلیس
4. ماشین آتش نشانی
5. آتش
6. آتش نشان
7. تانک
8. آزادی
9. سرباز

Auto

1
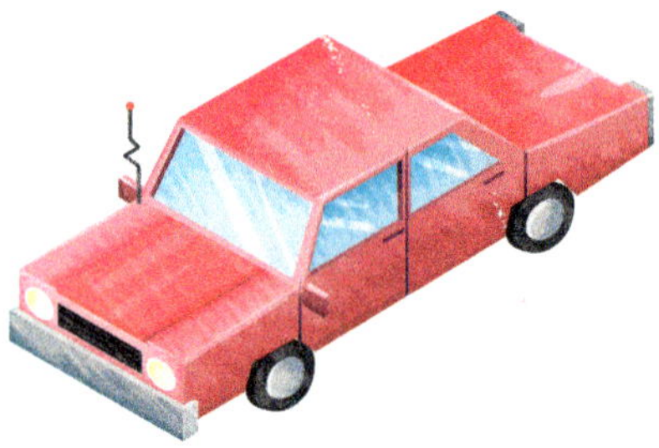
car

2

truck

3

motorcycle

4

semi-truck

5

garbage truck

6

taxi

7

to drive

8

fast

9

slow

1. خودرو
2. کامیون
3. موتورسیکلت
4. کامیونت
5. کامیون زباله
6. تاکسی
7. رانندگی کردن
8. سریع
9. آهسته

Auto

1

engine

2

windshield

3

headlight

4

steering wheel

5

bumper

6

tire

7

gas

8

to fill

9

empty

1. موتور
2. شیشه جلو اتوموبیل
3. چراغ جلو اتوموبیل
4. فرمان
5. سپر
6. لاستیک اتوموبیل
7. بنزین
8. پر کردن
9. خالی

Traffic

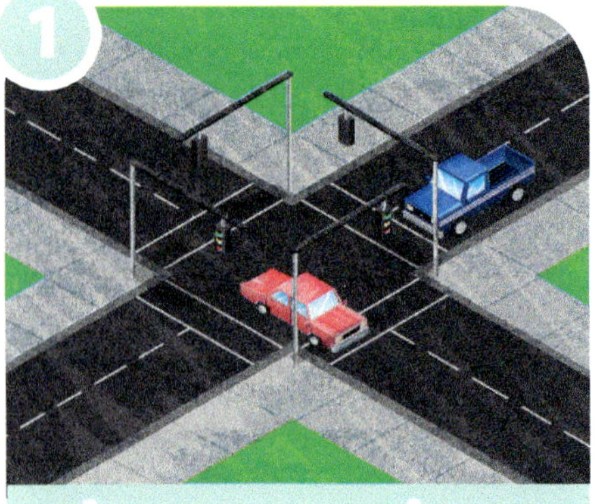

1 intersection

2 corner

3 sidewalk

4 crosswalk

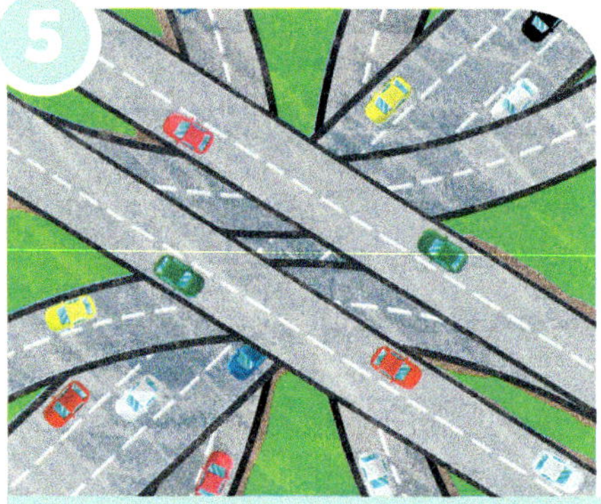

5 freeway

6 street

7 to crash

8 to park

9 to speed

1. تقاطع
2. گوشه
3. پیاده رو
4. خط عابر پیاده
5. اتوبان
6. خیابان
7. تصادف کردن
8. پارک کردن
9. با سرعت رفتن

Traffic

1

traffic

2

speed

3

careless

4

traffic light

5

sign

6

careful

7

to stop

8

to go

9

to cross

City

1. ترافیک 2. سرعت 3. بی دقت

4. چراغ راهنمایی رانندگی 5. علامت 6. با دقت

7. توقف کردن 8. رفتن 9. رد شدن

Traffic

1

train

2

subway

3

to get on

4

to get off

5

to wait

1. قطار
2. مترو
3. سوار شدن
4. پیاده شدن
5. صبر کردن

Jobs

1

trash collector

2

judge

3

mayor

4

mail carrier

5

driver

6

engineer

7

security

8

architect

9

lawyer

City

1. مسئول جمع آوری زباله 2. قاضی 3. شهردار

4. مامور پست 5. راننده 6. مهندس

7. مامور امنیتی 8. معمار 9. وکیل

Find Benny

Life

Benny wants the ball.

بنی توپ را می خواهد.

He never gets the ball.

او هیچ وقت توپ را نگرفته است.

Life

1

lazy

2

afraid

3

dishonest

4

smart

5

confident

6

creative

7

to relax

8

to want

9

to pray

1. تنبل
2. ترسیده
3. متقلب
4. باهوش
5. با اعتماد به نفس
6. خلاق
7. استراحت کردن
8. خواستن
9. دعا کردن

Restaurant

1

menu

2

chef

3

waiter

4

straw

5

lid

6

placemat

7

to order

8

drive-through

9

to ask

Life

1. منوی غذا
2. سرآشپز
3. گارسون
4. نی
5. درب ظرف
6. زیر بشقابی
7. سفارش دادن
8. رستوران درایو ترو
9. پرسیدن

Shopping

1

mall

2

store

3

to shop

4

groceries

5

cart

6

to pay

7

expensive

8

cheap

9

line

Life

1. مرکز خرید
2. مغازه
3. خرید کردن
4. خواربار فروشی
5. چرخ دستی خرید
6. پرداخت کردن
7. گران
8. ارزان
9. صف

Electronics

1

cell phone

2

camera

3
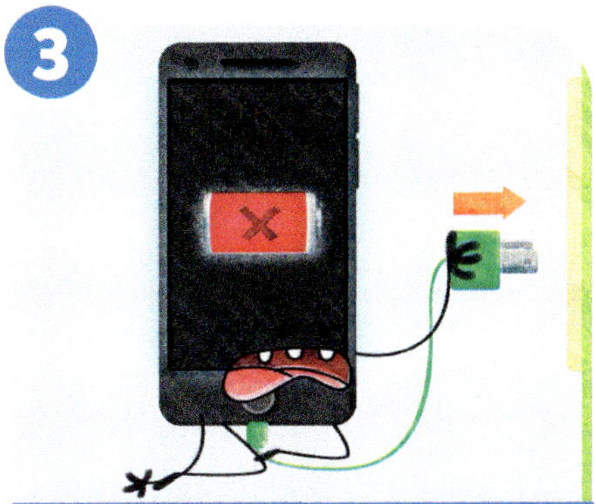
to charge

4

to call

5

to rewind

6

to fast forward

7

to send

8

to download

9

to record

1. تلفن همراه

2. دوربین

3. شارژ کردن

4. زنگ زدن

5. به عقب برگرداندن

6. به سرعت جلو زدن

7. فرستادن

8. دانلود کردن

9. ضبط کردن

Parks

1

swing

2

slide

3

monkey bars

4

picnic table

5

bench

6

to run

7

to climb

8

to push

9

to pull

1. تاب
2. سرسره
3. آویزگاه جنگلی
4. میز پیک نیک
5. نیمکت
6. دویدن
7. بالا رفتن
8. هل دادن
9. کشیدن

Parks

1

amusement park

2

water park

3

fair

4

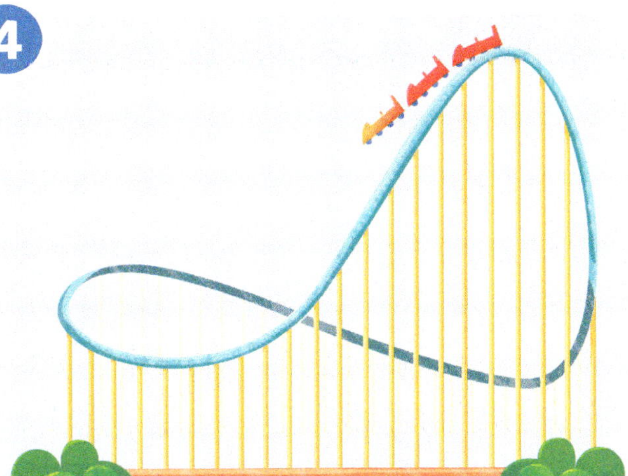

roller coaster

5

to ride

1. شهربازی
2. پارک آبی
3. نمایشگاه
4. ترن هوایی
5. سوار شدن

Sports

1

baseball

2

volleyball

3

basketball

4

football

5

soccer

6

hockey

7

referee

8

team

9

coach

1. بیسبال
2. والیبال
3. بسکتبال
4. فوتبال آمریکایی
5. فوتبال
6. هاکی
7. داور
8. تیم
9. مربی

Sports

1

surfing

2

wrestling

3

golf

4

track

5

skating

6

gymnastics

7

tennis

8

boxing

9

snowboarding

1. موج سواری

2. کشتی

3. گلف

4. دوومیدانی

5. اسکیت

6. ژیمناستیک

7. تنیس

8. بوکس

9. اسنوبورد

Sports

1

uniform

2

helmet

3

cleats

4

weights

5

shoulder pads

6

bat

7

to exercise

8

to practice

9

to stretch

Life

1. لباس فرم

2. کلاه ایمنی

3. کفش میخ دار

4. وزنه ها

5. بالشتک

6. چوب

7. ورزش کردن

8. تمرین کردن

9. کش و قوس آمدن

Sports

1 to win

2 to lose

3 to hit

4 to throw

5 to kick

6 to catch

7 to jump

8 to pass

9 to race

1. برنده شدن
2. باختن
3. ضربه زدن
4. پرتاب کردن
5. لگد زدن
6. گرفتن
7. پریدن
8. پاس دادن
9. مسابقه دادن

Music

1

guitar

2

drums

3

piano

4

violin

5

flute

6

trumpet

7

song

8

to sing

9

band

Life

1. گیتار
2. درام
3. پیانو

4. ویولون
5. فلوت
6. شیپور

7. آهنگ
8. آواز خواندن
9. گروه

1

concert

2

crowd

3

volume

4

high *(volume)*

5

low *(volume)*

1. کنسرت
2. جمعیت
3. درجه صدا
4. بلند
5. کم

Entertainment

movie

show

cartoon

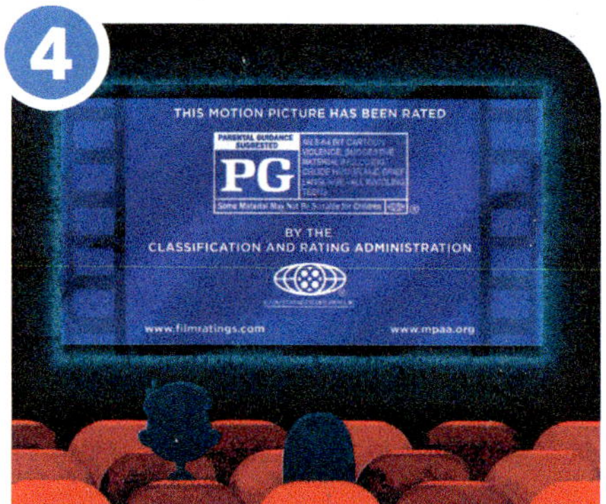

movie theater

bowling

arcade game

zoo

to like

to enjoy

1. فیلم سینمایی

2. برنامه تلویزیونی

3. کارتون

4. سینما

5. بولینگ

6. بازی آرکید

7. باغ وحش

8. پسندیدن

9. لذت بردن

Life

Holiday

1

New Years

2

Valentine's Day

3

Independence Day

4

Halloween

5

Thanksgiving

6

Christmas

7

fireworks

8

Easter

9

to decorate

Life

1. تعطیلات سال نو
2. ولنتاین
3. روز استقلال
4. هالووین
5. روز شکرگزاری
6. کریسمس
7. آتش بازی
8. عید پاک
9. تزیین کردن

Find the Object

Life

Chapter 9

Nature

Benny orders roses for Jenny.

بنی برای جنی گل سفارش داده است.

Jenny hates cactus.

او از کاکتوس متنفر است.

Plants

1

tree

2

bush

3

flower

4

branch

5

leaf

6

root

7

trunk

8

shade

9

to grow

Nature

1. درخت **2.** بوته **3.** گل

4. شاخه **5.** برگ **6.** ریشه

7. تنه **8.** سایه **9.** رشد کردن

Plants

1

cactus

2

palm tree

3

pine tree

4

rose

5

thorn

6

vine

7

seed

8

soil

9

to water

1. کاکتوس
2. درخت نخل
3. درخت کاج

4. گل رز
5. خار
6. درخت مو

7. دانه
8. خاک
9. آب دادن

Earth

1

Earth

2

land

3

mountain

4

desert

5

jungle

6

forest

7

island

8

hill

9

valley

Nature

1. زمین
2. خشکی
3. کوه
4. صحرا
5. جنگل
6. جنگل
7. جزیره
8. تپه
9. دره

Earth

1

ocean

2

river

3

lake

4

waterfall

5

beach

6

wave

7

mud

8

rock

9

sand

1. اقیانوس
2. رودخانه
3. دریاچه
4. آبشار
5. ساحل
6. موج
7. گل
8. صخره
9. شن

Space

1

planet

2

star

3

comet

4

sun

5

moon

6

satellite

7

austronaut

8

alien

9

to explore

1. سیاره
2. ستاره
3. ستاره دنباله دار
4. خورشید
5. ماه
6. ماهواره
7. فضانورد
8. موجودات فضایی
9. کاوش کردن

Time

1

day

2

night

3

morning

4

spring

5

summer

6

afternoon

7

fall

8

winter

9

evening

1. روز　**2.** شب　**3.** صبح

4. بهار　**5.** تابستان　**6.** بعدازظهر

7. پاییز　**8.** زمستان　**9.** عصر

Weather

1 rain

2 lightning

3 storm

4 sky

5 cloud

6 snow

7 umbrella

8 puddle

9 under

Nature

1. باران

2. رعد و برق

3. طوفان

4. آسمان

5. ابر

6. برف

7. چتر

8. چاله آب

9. زیر

Weather

1

hot

2

warm

3

cold

4

to melt

5

temperature

6

to freeze

7

sunny

8

cloudy

9

windy

1. داغ
2. گرم
3. سرد
4. ذوب کردن
5. دما
6. یخ زدن
7. آفتابی
8. ابری
9. طوفانی

Weather

1

tornado

2

volcano

3

earthquake

4

wildfire

5

tidal wave

6

flood

7

to help

8

to rescue

9

drought

1. گردباد
2. آتشفشان
3. زلزله
4. آتش سوزی شدید در جنگل
5. موج های بسیار بزرگ
6. سیل
7. کمک کردن
8. نجات دادن
9. خشکسالی

Environment

1

to recycle

2

to litter

3

to use

4

to waste

5

pollution

1. بازیافت کردن

2. آشغال ریختن

3. استفاده کردن

4. اسراف کردن

5. آلودگی

Leaf Art

Go outside! Find some interesting looking leaves and enjoy the sun.

1. Find leaves of different shapes and sizes.

2. Place a thin sheet of paper over one leaf.

3. Gently rub the side of a crayon on the area over the leaf.

4. Rub the crayon over the entire leaf.

5. Repeat with another leaf and different color.

6. Cover the sheet of paper with different leaves and colors.

Benny talks to the animals.

بنی با حیوانات حرف می زند.

The animals talk back.

حیوانات هم با او حرف می زنند.

Farm

1

cow

2

pig

3

chicken

4

donkey

5

horse

6

turkey

7

goat

8

sheep

9

farm

1. گاو
2. خوک
3. مرغ
4. الاغ
5. اسب
6. بوقلمون
7. بز
8. گوسفند
9. مزرعه

Ocean

1

fish

2

shark

3

squid

4

octopus

5

crab

6

whale

7

dolphin

8

seal

9

to swim

1. ماهی
2. کوسه
3. ماهی مرکب
4. هشت پا
5. خرچنگ
6. نهنگ
7. دلفین
8. فوک دریایی
9. شنا کردن

Forest

1

raccoon

2

skunk

3

porcupine

4

deer

5

bear

6

wolf

7

fur

8

cave

9

to howl

1. راکون
2. راسو
3. جوجه تیغی
4. آهو
5. خرس
6. گرگ
7. خز
8. غار
9. زوزه کشیدن

Jungle

1

panda

2

lion

3

crocodile

4

monkey

5

elephant

6

snake

7

giraffe

8

fang

9

zebra

1. پاندا
2. شیر
3. کروکدیل
4. میمون
5. فیل
6. مار
7. زرافه
8. گرگ
9. گورخر

Bird

1

bird

2

wing

3

feather

4

duck

5

owl

6

beak

7

penguin

8

eagle

9

nest

Animals

1. پرنده
2. بال
3. پر
4. اردک
5. جغد
6. منقار
7. پنگوئن
8. عقاب
9. لانه

Insects

1

insect

2

ant

3

fly

4

bee

5

snail

6

spider

7

hive

8

shell

9

web

1. حشره
2. مورچه
3. مگس
4. زنبور
5. حلزون
6. عنکبوت
7. کندو
8. صدف حلزون
9. تار عنکبوت

Pets

1

dog

2

puppy

3

to bark

4

cat

5

kitten

6

to meow

7

leash

8

collar

9

tail

1. سگ
2. توله سگ
3. پارس کردن
4. گربه
5. بچه گربه
6. میو میو کردن
7. بند قلاده
8. قلاده
9. دم

Pets

1

to pet

2

to feed

3

to walk

4

to chase

1. پیاده روی کردن

2. غذا دادن

3. نوازش کردن

4. دنبال کردن

5. آموزش دادن

5

to train

Animals

Build Benny

Download Benny the Bear at:
www.bilingualbear.com

1. Fold the paper in half along the dotted line.

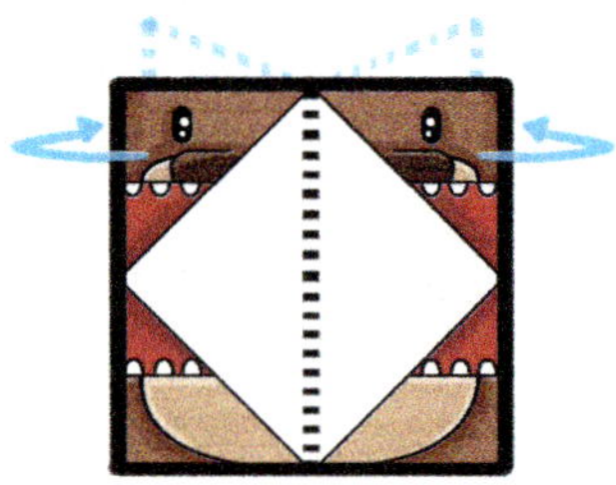

2. Flip the page over. Fold the corners in.

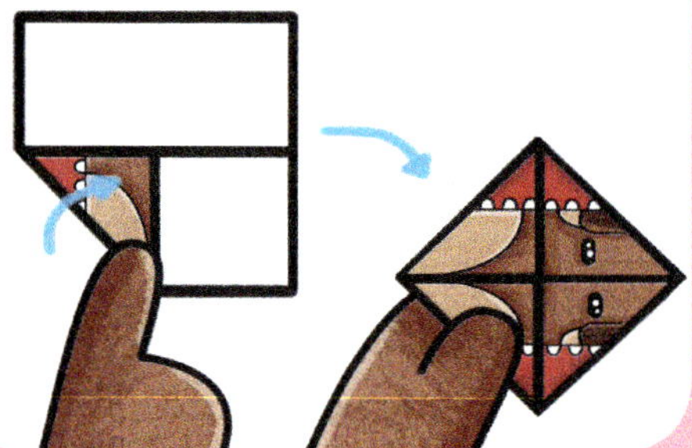

3. Flip the page over. Fold the corners in again.

4. Fold the square in half, both ways.

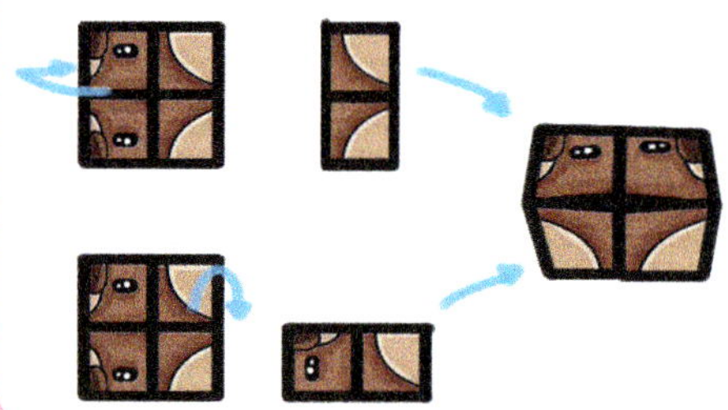

5. Place your fingers under the four open corners and pinch the paper to open up Benny's face.

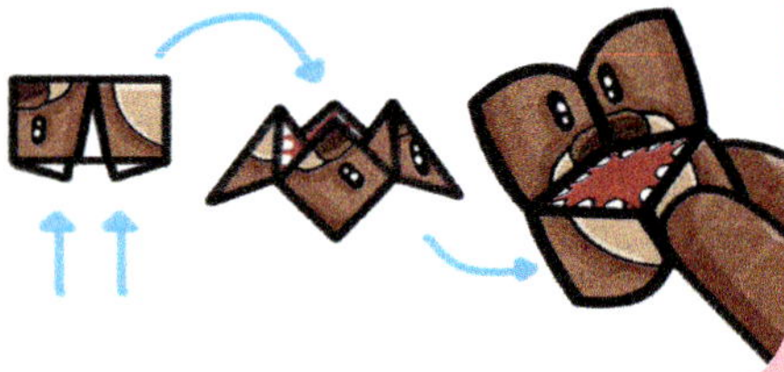

6. Glue Benny's body onto the Benny's face.

Animals

More Words

Chapter 11

Benny is a fun bear. Benny knows life is more fun if you know the right words. After school, he loves to learn new words. Benny's mother yells, "Do your homework!" Benny says, "Yes mother, I am."

بنی خرس باحالی است. بنی می داند
که اگر کلمات درست را بلد باشد
زندگی باحال تر هم می شود. بعد از
مدرسه، او دوست دارد که کلمات
جدید را یاد بگیرد. مادر بنی داد می
زند: «مشق هایت را بنویس!» و بنی
جواب می دهد: «چشم مادر.»

Numbers

0	1	2	3
zero صفر	one یک	two دو	three سه
4	5	6	7
four چهار	five پنج	six شش	seven هفت
8	9	10	11
eight هشت	nine نه	ten ده	eleven یازده
12	13	14	15
twelve دوازده	thirteen سیزده	fourteen چهارده	fifteen پانزده
16	17	18	19
sixteen شانزده	seventeen هفده	eighteen هجده	nineteen نوزده
20	30	40	50
twenty بیست	thirty سی	forty چهل	fifty پنجاه
60	70	80	90
sixty شصت	seventy هفتاد	eighty هشتاد	ninety نود

Money

dollar
دلار

penny
پنی

nickel
نیکل

dime
سکه ده سنتی

quarter
ربع

fifty-five cents
چهل و پنج سنت

thirty-three cents
سی و سه سنت

one dollar and twenty-six cents
یک دلار و بیست و شش سنت

100
one hundred
صد

200
two hundred
دویست

1000
one thousand
هزار

2000
two thousand
دوهزار

Time

sunrise
طلوع آفتاب

sunset
غروب آفتاب

twelve o' clock
ساعت دوازده

noon
ظهر

midnight
نیمه شب

one fifteen
یک و پانزده دقیقه

quarter past one
یک و ربع

one thirty
یک و سی دقیقه

half past one
یک و نیم

one forty-five
یک و چهل و پنج دقیقه

quarter to two
یک ربع به دو

Colors

purple	بنفش
blue	آبی
green	سبز
yellow	زرد
orange	نارنجی
red	قرمز
pink	صورتی
black	سیاه
white	سفید
gray	خاکستری
brown	قهوه ای
tan	برنزه
gold	طلایی
silver	نقره ای

Shapes

square
مربع

rectangle
مستطیل

triangle
مثلث

circle
دایره

oval
بیضی

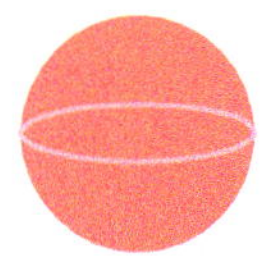

sphere
کره

cube
مکعب

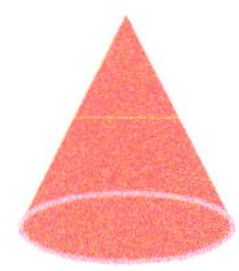

cone
مخروط

heart
قلب

cross
صلیب

arrow
کمان

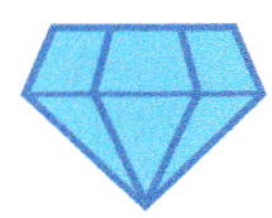

diamond
الماس

star
ستاره

line
خط

up
بالا

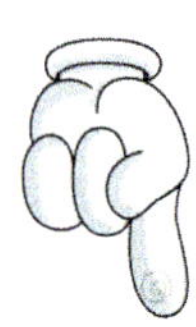

down
پایین

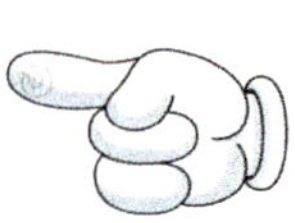

left
چپ

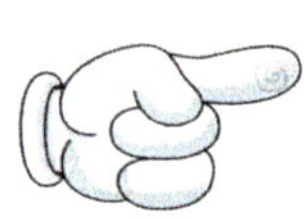

right
راست

Glossary

A

to add ... 84
adult ... 10
afraid ... 106
afternoon ... 127
airport ... 92
alien ... 126
allergy ... 74
alone ... 29
alphabet ... 86
ambulance ... 95
amusement park ... 111
angry ... 73
ankle ... 69
ant ... 139
apartment ... 16
apple ... 58
arcade game ... 118
architect ... 103
arm ... 68
arrow ... 148
to ask ... 107
astronaut ... 126
atom ... 85
auditorium ... 78
aunt ... 8
auto shop ... 93
author ... 94
avocado ... 58
awake ... 23

B

baby ... 10
back ... 69
backpack ... 88
bacon ... 52
bag ... 31
to bake ... 49
balloon ... 12
banana ... 58
band ... 116
bank ... 93
barbecue ... 30
barbecue sauce ... 57
to bark ... 140
baseball ... 112
baseball cap ... 39
basket ... 44
basketball ... 112
bat ... 114
bathroom ... 19
bathtub ... 24
beach ... 125
beak ... 138
beans ... 55
bear ... 136
bed ... 22
bedroom ... 19
bee ... 139
belt ... 40
bench ... 110
beverage ... 50
bikini ... 38
bird ... 138
birthday ... 12
to bite ... 67
black ... 147
blanket ... 22
to bleed ... 71
to blend ... 49
blood ... 71
bloody ... 75
blue ... 147
blueberry ... 58
board game ... 28
body ... 68
to boil ... 49
bone ... 71
book ... 94
boots ... 37
bowl ... 21
bowling ... 118
box ... 31
boxing ... 113
boy ... 10
bracelet ... 40
brain ... 70
branch ... 122
bread ... 48
to break ... 32
breakfast ... 50
to breathe ... 70
bride ... 13
bridge ... 93

broccoli 60
broken 75
broom 33
brother 8
brown 147
browser 83
bruise 75
to brush 26
bucket 33
bumper 99
burn 75
to burp 62
burrito 53
bus 81
bus stop 93
bush 122
butter 52
button 40

C

cactus 123
cafeteria 78
cake 12
calculator 84
to call 109
camera 109
candle 12
car 98
careful 101
careless 101
carpet 27
carrot 60
to carry 31
cart 108
cartoon 118
cat 140
to catch 115
cave 136
ceiling 27
celery 60
cell 85
cell phone 109
cereal 52
to charge 109
to chase 141
cheap 108
check 96
to check out 94
cheek 66
to cheer 29
cheese 54
chef 107
cherry 59
chest 69
to chew 62
chicken 55
chicken 134
chicken nugget 53
child 10
children 9
chimney 17
chin 67
chips 56
chocolate 56
Christmas 119
church 92
circle 148
city 92
city hall 92
classmate 79
classroom 78
clean 25
cleats 114
to climb 110
clock 80
to close 26
closet 22
cloud 128
cloudy 129
coach 112
coconut 59
coffee 51
cold 74
cold 129
collar 140
college 81
to color 89
comb 24
to comb 26
comet 126
comfortable 29
computer 82
concert 117

condiments . . . 48
cone . . . 148
confident . . . 106
controller . . . 28
to cook . . . 21
cookie . . . 56
cooler . . . 31
corndog . . . 53
corner . . . 100
costume . . . 41
couch . . . 27
to cough . . . 74
counter . . . 20
court house . . . 93
cousin . . . 8
cow . . . 134
cowboy hat . . . 41
crab . . . 135
to crash . . . 100
crayon . . . 88
creative . . . 106
crime . . . 97
crocodile . . . 137
to cross . . . 101
cross . . . 148
crosswalk . . . 100
crowd . . . 117
crutch . . . 95
to cry . . . 13
cube . . . 148
cucumber . . . 60
cup . . . 21
cupboard . . . 20
cupcake . . . 56
cut . . . 75
to cut . . . 89

D

to dance . . . 13
data . . . 85
day . . . 127
debit card . . . 96
to decorate . . . 119
deer . . . 136
delicious . . . 63
dentist . . . 95
to deposit . . . 96
desert . . . 124
desk . . . 80
dessert . . . 50
detergent . . . 44
diamond . . . 148
difficult . . . 87
dime . . . 145
dinner . . . 50
to dip . . . 57
dirty . . . 25
dishonest . . . 106
dishwasher . . . 20
to divide . . . 84
doctor . . . 95
dog . . . 140
dog house . . . 30
dollar . . . 96
dolphin . . . 135
donkey . . . 134
donut . . . 56
door . . . 16
doorbell . . . 16
doorknob . . . 16
down . . . 148
to download . . . 109
dream . . . 23
dress . . . 38
dresser . . . 22
to drink . . . 62
to drive . . . 98
driver . . . 103
drive-through . . . 107
drought . . . 130
drums . . . 116
dry . . . 25
dryer . . . 44
duck . . . 138
dustpan . . . 33
DVD player . . . 28

Glossary

E

eagle 138
ear 66
earring 40
Earth 124
earthquake 130
Easter 119
easy 87
to eat 62
egg 52
eight 144
eighteen 144
eighty 145
elbow 68
electricity 85
elementary 81
elephant 137
eleven 144
email 83
embarrassed 73
emergency 95
to empty 33
empty 99
energy 85
engine 99
engineer 103
to enjoy 118
to erase 89
eraser 88
even 84
evening 127
excited 73
to exercise 114
expensive 108
experiment 85
to explore 126
extra large 42
eye 66
eyebrow 66

F

face 66
fair 111
to fall 31
fall 127
fan 31
fang 137
farm 134
fast 98
to fast forward 109
fat 11
father 8
faucet 24
feather 138
to feed 141
fence 17
fever 74
field 78
fifteen 144
fifty 145
fifty-five cents 145
to fill 99
finger 68
fire 97
fire fighter 97
fire station 92
fire truck 97
fireplace 27
fireworks 119
fish 135
fish sticks 53
five 144
to fix 32
flag 80
flash drive 82
flood 130
floor 27
floss 25
flower 122
flu 74
flute 116
fly 139
to fold 45
foot 69
football 112
forehead 66
forest 124
to forget 87
fork 21
forty 145
fountain 78
four 144

fourteen 144
freedom 97
freeway 100
to freeze 129
fresh 61
friends 12
fries 53
frosting 56
fruit 48
to fry 49
full 63
fun 12
fur 136

G

game 12
garage 17
garbage truck 98
garden 30
gas 99
gas station 93
gate 17
to get off 102
to get on 102
gift 12
giraffe 137
girl 10
glove 41
glue 88
to glue 89
to go 101
goat 134
gold 147
golf 113
to graduate 81
grandfather 8
grandmother 8
grapes 58
graph 84
green 147
gray 147
to grill 49
groceries 108
groom 13
to grow 122
guard 79
guitar 116
gymnasium 78
gymnastics 113

H

hair 66
half past one 146
Halloween 119
ham 52
hamburger 53
hammer 32
hamper 24
hand 68
handsome 11
to hang 45
hanger 44
happy 73
hat 36
head 66
headache 74
headlight 99
healthy 69
to hear 72
heart 71
heart 148
heel 37
helmet 114
to help 130
high 117
high school 81
hill 124
hips 69
to hit 115
hive 139
hockey 112
homework 87
horse 134
hose 30
hospital 92
hot 129
hotdog 53
house 16
to howl 136
to hug 13
hungry 63
husband and wife 9

Glossary

Glossary

I

ice 51
ice cream 56
Independence Day 119
insect 139
internet 83
intersection 100
to invite 18
iron 44
to iron 44
island 124

J

jacket 36
janitor 79
jeans 39
jelly 54
judge 103
juice 51
juicy 59
to jump 115
jungle 124
junk food 56

K

ketchup 57
key 16
keyboard 82
to kick 115
to kiss 13
kitchen 19
kitten 140
knee 69
knife 21
to knock 16

L

ladder 31
lake 125
lamp 22
land 124
language 86
laptop 82
large 42
to laugh 13
laundry 44
lawn 30
lawn mower 30
lawyer 103
lazy 106
leaf 122
to learn 81
leash 140
left 148
leg 69
lemon 59
lemonade 51
lesson 87
letter 86
lettuce 60
librarian 94
library 92
library card 94
to lick 62
lid 107
lightning 128
to like 118
lime 59
line 108
line 148
link 83
lion 137
lips 67
to listen 79
to litter 131
living room 19
locker 78
to login 83
loose 43
to lose 115
lotion 25
loud 80
to love 13
low 117
lunch 50
lunchbox 54
lungs 70

M

magazine . . . 94
mail . . . 17
mail carrier . . . 103
mailbox . . . 17
make-up . . . 38
mall . . . 108
man . . . 10
mango . . . 59
marker . . . 80
math . . . 84
mayonnaise . . . 57
mayor . . . 103
to measure . . . 89
meat . . . 48
medicine . . . 95
medium . . . 42
to meet . . . 18
to melt . . . 129
menu . . . 107
to meow . . . 140
microwave . . . 20
middle school . . . 81
midnight . . . 146
milk . . . 51
mirror . . . 24
money . . . 96
monitor . . . 82
monkey . . . 137
monkey bars . . . 110
moon . . . 126
mop . . . 33
morning . . . 127
mother . . . 8
motorcycle . . . 98
mountain . . . 124
mouse . . . 82
mouth . . . 67
movie . . . 118
movie theater . . . 118
mud . . . 125
to multiply . . . 84
muscle . . . 71
museum . . . 93
mushroom . . . 60
mustard . . . 57

N

nail . . . 32
nail . . . 68
neck . . . 67
necklace . . . 40
neighbor . . . 18
nest . . . 138
new . . . 43
New Years . . . 119
newspaper . . . 94
nickel . . . 145
niece and nephew . . . 9
night . . . 127
night-light . . . 22
nightmare . . . 23
nightstand . . . 22
nine . . . 144
nineteen . . . 144
ninety . . . 145
noon . . . 146
nose . . . 66
nurse . . . 79

O

oatmeal . . . 52
to observe . . . 85
ocean . . . 125
octopus . . . 135
odd . . . 84
off . . . 28
office . . . 78
old . . . 11
on . . . 28
one . . . 144
one dollar and twenty-six cents . . . 145
one fifteen . . . 146
one forty-five . . . 146
one hundred . . . 145
one thirty . . . 146
one thousand . . . 145
onion . . . 60
to open . . . 26
orange . . . 59
orange . . . 147
to order . . . 107

Glossary

organic 61
oval 148
oven 20
owl 138

P

pain 75
paint 31
painting 27
pajamas 41
palm tree 123
pan 49
pancakes 52
panda 137
pants 36
paper 88
parents 9
to park 100
parking lot 93
party 12
to pass 115
password 83
patient 95
to pay 108
peanut butter 54
to peel 49
pen 88
pencil 88
penguin 138
penny 145
to pet 141
piano 116
pickle 60
picnic table 110
pie 56
pig 134
pillow 22
pin number 96
pine tree 123
pineapple 58
pink 147
pizza 53
placemat 107
planet 126
plate 21
to play 18
playground 78
police car 97
police officer 97
police station 92
polka dot 42
pollution 131
porcupine 136
post office 92
poster 22
pot 49
to pour 57
power drill 32
to practice 114
to pray 106
to prepare 21
pretty 11
principal 79
printer 82
processed 61
projector 80
proud 73
puddle 128
to pull 110
pumpkin 58
puppy 140
purple 147
purse 38
to push 110
to put 45
to put on 37

Q

quarter 145
quarter past one 146
quarter *to* two 146
question 86
quiet 80

R

raccoon 136
to race 115
radio 28
rain 128
raisin 59

rash 75
to read 86
to receive 17
to record 109
rectangle 148
to recycle 131
recycle bin 31
red 147
referee 112
refrigerator 20
to relax 106
report 87
to rescue 130
to respect 79
to return 94
to rewind 109
rice 55
to ride 111
right 148
to ring 16
ring 40
ripe 61
river 125
rock 125
roller coaster 111
roof 17
root 122
rose 123
rotten 61
ruler 88
to run 110

S

sad 73
salad 55
salad dressing 57
salt 57
sand 125
sandals 37
sandwich 53
satellite 126
sausage 52
to save 96
scared 73
scarf 40
science 85
scientist 85
scissors 88
screen 80
screwdriver 32
to scrub 33
seal 135
to search 83
security 103
to see 72
seed 123
semi-truck 98
to send 109
senior 10
sentence 86
seven 144
seventeen 144
seventy 145
shade 122
shark 135
sheep 134
shell 139
shirt 36
shoelaces 37
shoes 36
to shop 108
short 11
shorts 36
shoulder 68
shoulder pads 114
show 118
shower 24
to shower 26
shy 73
sidewalk 100
sign 101
silver 147
to sing 116
sink 20
sister 8
six 144
sixteen 144
sixty 145
skating 113
skeleton 71
skirt 38
skull 71
skunk 136

sky 128
to sleep 23
sleepy 23
sliced 59
slide 110
slow 98
small 42
smart 106
to smell 72
to smile 67
snacks 54
snail 139
snake 137
sneakers 37
to sneeze 74
snow 128
snowboarding 113
soap 24
soccer 112
sock 36
soda 51
soil 123
soldier 97
sole 37
solid 42
son and daughter 9
song 116
soup 55
spaghetti 55
speaker 82
to speed 100
speed 101
sphere 148
spicy 63
spider 139
sponge 33
spoon 21
sprained 75
spring 127
to sprinkle 57
sprinkler 30
square 148
squid 135
stained 42
stairs 17
star 126
star 148
steak 55
steering wheel 99
to stir 49
stomach 70
stomach ache 74
to stop 101
store 108
storm 128
stove 20
straw 107
strawberry 58
street 100
to stretch 114
striped 42
strong 71
student 79
to study 81
style 43
to subtract 84
subway 102
summer 127
sun 126
sunny 129
sunrise 146
sunset 146
surfing 113
surprised 73
sushi 55
sweater 36
to sweep 33
sweet 63
to swim 135
swimming trunks 39
swings 110
switch 27
swollen 75

T

table 27
tail 140
to take off 37
tall 11
tan 147
tank 97
tape 32
to taste 72

taxi . . . 98
tea . . . 51
to teach . . . 81
teacher . . . 79
team . . . 112
teenager . . . 10
teeth . . . 67
television . . . 28
teller . . . 96
temperature . . . 129
ten . . . 144
tennis . . . 113
test . . . 87
textbook . . . 87
Thanksgiving . . . 119
thin . . . 11
to think . . . 70
thirsty . . . 51
thirteen . . . 144
thirty . . . 145
thirty-three cents . . . 145
thorn . . . 123
three . . . 144
to throw . . . 115
thumb . . . 68
tidal wave . . . 130
to tie . . . 37
tight . . . 43
tire . . . 99
title . . . 94
toast . . . 52
toaster . . . 20
toe . . . 69
together . . . 29
toilet . . . 24
toilet paper . . . 24
tomato . . . 60
tongue . . . 67
toolbox . . . 32
toothbrush . . . 25
toothpaste . . . 25
torn . . . 42
tornado . . . 130
tortilla . . . 55
to touch . . . 72
towel . . . 25
toy . . . 28
track . . . 113
traffic . . . 101
traffic light . . . 101
train . . . 102
to train . . . 141
trash can . . . 30
trash collector . . . 103
tree . . . 122
tree house . . . 30
triangle . . . 148
truck . . . 98
trumpet . . . 116
trunk . . . 122
to try . . . 45
t-shirt . . . 39
tunnel . . . 93
turkey . . . 134
to turn-in . . . 87
twelve . . . 144
twelve o'clock . . . 146
twenty . . . 144
two . . . 144
two hundred . . . 145
two thousand . . . 145
to type . . . 86

U

ugly . . . 11
umbrella . . . 128
uncle . . . 8
under . . . 128
underwear . . . 36
uniform . . . 41
uniform . . . 114
up . . . 148
USB port . . . 82
to use . . . 131
used . . . 43
username . . . 83

V

vacuum . . . 33
Valentine's Day . . . 119
valley . . . 124
vegetable . . . 48

Glossary

video game . . . 28
vine . . . 123
violin . . . 116
volcano . . . 130
volleyball . . . 112
volume . . . 117
to vomit . . . 74

W

to wait . . . 102
waiter . . . 107
to walk . . . 141
wall . . . 27
wallet . . . 39
to want . . . 106
warm . . . 129
to wash . . . 21
washer . . . 44
to waste . . . 131
to watch . . . 29
watch . . . 40
water . . . 51
to water . . . 123
water park . . . 111
waterfall . . . 125
watermelon . . . 58
to wave . . . 18
wave . . . 125
weak . . . 71
to wear . . . 45
web . . . 139
website . . . 83
wedding . . . 13
weights . . . 114
wet . . . 25
whale . . . 135
wheelchair . . . 95
white . . . 147
whiteboard . . . 80
wildfire . . . 130
to win . . . 115
window . . . 16
windshield . . . 99
windy . . . 129
wing . . . 138
to wink . . . 67
winter . . . 127
to withdraw . . . 96
wolf . . . 136
woman . . . 10
word . . . 86
wrench . . . 32
wrestling . . . 113
wrinkled . . . 44
wrist . . . 68
to write . . . 86

X

x-ray . . . 95

Y

yard . . . 19
yellow . . . 147
young . . . 11

Z

zebra . . . 137
zero . . . 144
zipper . . . 40
zoo . . . 118